180 Days of Social-Emotional Learning for Kindergarten

Jodene Lynn Smith, M.A.

Brenda Van Dixhorn, M.A.Ed.

Consultants

Kris Hinrichsen, M.A.T., NBCT
Teacher and Educational Consultant
Anchorage School District

Amy Zoque
Teacher and Instructional Coach
Ontario Montclair School District

Publishing Credits

Corinne Burton, M.A.Ed., *Publisher*
Emily R. Smith, M.A.Ed., *VP of Content Development*
Lynette Ordoñez, *Content Specialist*
David Slayton, *Assistant Editor*
Jill Malcolm, *Multimedia Specialist*

Image Credits: all images from iStock and/or Shutterstock

Social-Emotional Learning Framework

The CASEL SEL framework and competencies were used in the development of this series.
© 2020 The Collaborative for Academic, Social, and Emotional Learning

Shell Education
A division of Teacher Created Materials
5482 Argosy Avenue
Huntington Beach, CA 92649-1039
www.tcmpub.com/shell-education
ISBN 978-1-0876-4969-6
© 2022 Shell Educational Publishing, Inc.

Table of Contents

Introduction

"SEL is the process through which all young people and adults acquire and apply the knowledge, skills, and attitudes to develop healthy identities, manage emotions and achieve personal and collective goals, feel and show empathy for others, establish and maintain supportive relationships, and make responsible and caring decisions." (CASEL 2020)

Social-emotional learning (SEL) covers a wide range of skills that help people improve themselves and get fulfilment from their relationships. They are the skills that help propel us into the people we want to be. SEL skills give people the tools to think about the future and manage the day-to-day goal setting to get where we want to be.

The National Commission for Social, Emotional, and Academic Development (2018) noted that children need many skills, attitudes, and values to succeed in school, future careers, and life. "They require skills such as paying attention, setting goals, collaboration and planning for the future. They require attitudes such as internal motivation, perseverance, and a sense of purpose. They require values such as responsibility, honesty, and integrity. They require the abilities to think critically, consider different views, and problem solve." Explicit SEL instruction will help students develop and hone these important skills, attitudes, and values.

Daniel Goleman (2005), a social scientist who popularized SEL, adds, "Most of us have assumed that the kind of academic learning that goes on in school has little or nothing to do with one's emotions or social environment. Now, neuroscience is telling us exactly the opposite. The emotional centers of the brain are intricately interwoven with the neocortical areas involved in cognitive learning." As adults, we may find it difficult to focus on work after a bad day or a traumatic event. Similarly, student learning is impacted by their emotions. By teaching students how to deal with their emotions in a healthy way, they will reap the benefits academically as well.

SEL is doing the work to make sure students can be successful at home, with their friends, at school, in sports, in relationships, and in life. The skills are typically separated into five competencies: self-awareness, self-management, social awareness, relationship skills, and responsible decision-making.

Introduction *(cont.)*

Social-Emotional Competencies

SELF-MANAGEMENT
Manage your emotions, thoughts, and behaviors. Set and work toward goals.

SOCIAL AWARENESS
Take on the perspectives of others, especially those who are different from you. Understand societal expectations and know where to get support.

SEL COMPETENCIES

SELF-AWARENESS
Recognize your own emotions, thoughts, and values. Assess your strengths and weaknesses. Have a growth mindset.

RESPONSIBLE DECISION-MAKING
Make positive choices based on established norms. Understand and consider consequences.

RELATIONSHIP SKILLS
Establish and maintain relationships with others. Communicate effectively and negotiate conflict as necessary.

Each SEL competency helps support child development in life-long learning. SEL helps students develop the skills to have rich connections with their emotional lives and build robust emotional vocabularies. These competencies lead to some impressive data to support students being successful in school and in life.

- Students who learn SEL skills score an average of 11 percentage points higher on standardized tests.

- They are less likely to get office referrals and will spend more time in class.

- These students are more likely to want to come to school and report being happier while at school.

- Educators who teach SEL skills report a 77 percent increase in job satisfaction. (Durlack, et al. 2011)

Your SEL Skills

Educators, parents, and caretakers have a huge part to play as students develop SEL skills. Parker Palmer (2007) reminds us that what children do is often a reflection of what they see and experience. When you stay calm, name your feelings, practice clear communication, and problem-solve in a way that students see, then they reflect that modeling in their own relationships. As you guide students in how to handle conflicts, you can keep a growth mindset and know that with practice, your students can master any skill.

Introduction *(cont.)*

Scenarios

There are many benefits to teaching SEL, from how students behave at home to how they will succeed in life. Let's think about how children with strong SEL skills would react to common life experiences.

At Home

Kyle wakes up. He uses self-talk and says to himself, *I am going to do my best today.* He gets out of bed, picks out his own clothes to wear, and gets ready. As he sits down for breakfast, his little sister knocks over his glass of milk. He thinks, *Uggh, she is so messy! But that's ok—it was just an accident.* Then, he tells his parent and helps clean up the mess.

When his parent picks Kyle up from school, Kyle asks how they are feeling and answers questions about how his day has gone. He says that he found the reading lesson hard, but he used deep breathing and asked questions to figure out new words today.

As his family is getting dinner ready, he sees that his parent is making something he really doesn't like. He stomps his foot in protest, and then he goes to sit in his room for a while. When he comes out, he asks if they can make something tomorrow that he likes.

When he is getting ready for bed, he is silly and playful. He wants to read and point out how each person in the book is feeling. His parent asks him how he would handle the problem the character is facing, and then they talk about the situation.

At School

Cynthia gets to school a little late, and she has to check into the office. Cynthia is embarrassed about being late but feels safe at school and knows that the people there will welcome her with kindness. She steps into her room, and her class pauses to welcome her. Her teacher says, "I'm so glad you are here today."

Cynthia settles into her morning work. After a few minutes, she comes to a problem she doesn't know how to solve. After she gives it her best try, she asks her teacher for some help. Her teacher supports her learning, and Cynthia feels proud of herself for trying.

As lunchtime nears, Cynthia realizes she forgot her lunch in the car. She asks her teacher to call her mom. Her mom says she can't get away and that Cynthia is going to have to eat the school lunch today. Cynthia is frustrated but decides that she is not going to let it ruin her day.

As she is getting ready for school to end, her teacher invites the class to reflect about their day. What is something they are proud of? What is something they wished they could do again? Cynthia thinks about her answers and shares with the class.

These are both pretty dreamy children. The reality is that the development of SEL skills happens in different ways. Some days, students will shock you by how they handle a problem. Other times, they will dig in and not use the skills you teach them. One of the benefits of teaching SEL is that when a student is melting down, your mindset shifts to *I wonder how I can help them learn how to deal with this* rather than *I'm going to punish them so they don't do this again.* Viewing discipline as an opportunity to teach rather than punish is critical for students to learn SEL.

How to Use This Book

Using the Practice Pages

This series is designed to support the instruction of SEL. It is not a curriculum. The activities will help students practice, learn, and grow their SEL skills. Each week is set up for students to practice all five SEL competencies.

 Day 1—Self-Awareness

 Day 2—Self-Management

 Day 3—Social Awareness

 Day 4—Relationship Skills

 Day 5—Responsible Decision-Making

Each of the five competencies has subcategories that are used to target specific skills each day. See the chart on pages 10–11 for a list of which skills are used throughout the book.

Each week also has a theme. These themes rotate and are repeated several times throughout the book. The following themes are included in this book:

- self
- friends
- family
- neighborhood
- school

This book also features one week that focuses on online safety.

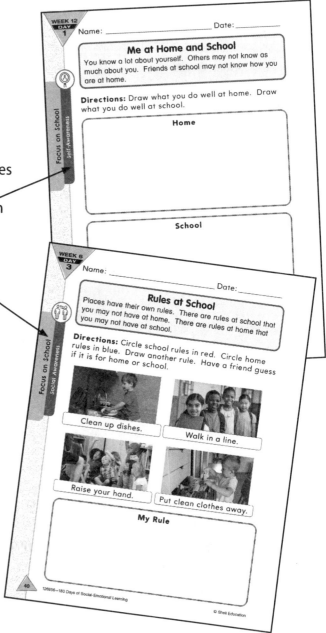

How to Use This Book *(cont.)*

Using the Resources

Rubrics for connecting to self, relating to others, and making decisions can be found on pages 197–199 and in the Digital Resources. Use the rubrics to consider student work. Be sure to share these rubrics with students so that they know what is expected of them.

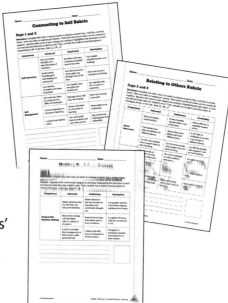

Diagnostic Assessment

Educators can use the pages in this book as diagnostic assessments. The data analysis tools included with this book enable teachers or parents/caregivers to quickly assess students' work and monitor their progress. Educators can quickly see which skills students may need to target further to develop proficiency.

Students will learn how to connect with their own emotions, how to connect with the emotions of others, and how to make good decisions. Assess student learning in each area using the rubrics on pages 197–199. Then, record their overall progress on the analysis sheets on pages 200–202. These charts are also provided in the Digital Resources as PDFs and Microsoft Excel® files.

To Complete the Analyses:

- Write or type students' names in the far-left column. Depending on the number of students, more than one copy of each form may be needed.

- The weeks in which students should be assessed are indicated in the first rows of the charts. Students should be assessed at the ends of those weeks.

- Review students' work for the day(s) indicated in the corresponding rubric. For example, if using the Making Decisions Analysis sheet for the first time, review students' work from Day 5 for all six weeks.

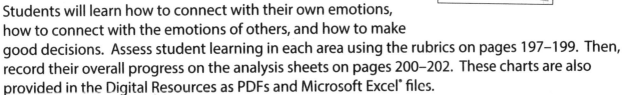

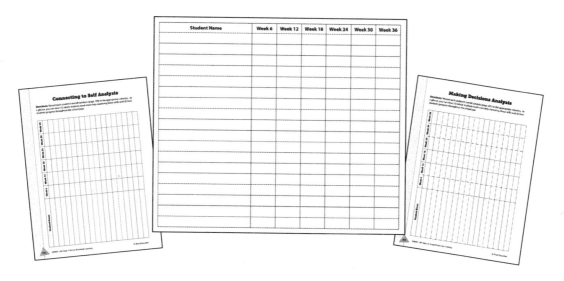

Integrating SEL into Your Teaching

Student self-assessment is key for SEL skills. If students can make accurate evaluations of how they are feeling, then they can work to manage their emotions. If they can manage their emotions, they are more likely to have better relationship skills and make responsible decisions. Children can self-assess from a very young age. The earlier you get them into this practice, the more they will use it and benefit from it for the rest of their lives. The following are some ways you can quickly and easily integrate student self-assessment into your daily routines.

Feelings Check-Ins

Using a scale can be helpful for a quick check-in. After an activity, ask students to rate how they are feeling. Focusing students' attention on how they are feeling helps support their self-awareness. Discuss how students' feelings change as they do different things. Provide students with a visual scale to support these check-ins. These could be taped to their desks or posted in your classroom. Full-color versions of the following scales can be found in the Digital Resources.

- **Emoji:** Having students point to different emoji faces is an easy way to use a rating scale with young students.

- **Symbols:** Symbols, such as weather icons, can also represent students' emotions.

- **Color Wheel:** A color wheel, where different colors represent different emotions, is another effective scale.

- **Numbers:** Have students show 1–5 fingers, with 5 being *I'm feeling great* to 1 being *I'm feeling awful*.

Integrating SEL into Your Teaching *(cont.)*

Reflection

Reflecting is the process of looking closely or deeply at something. When you prompt students with reflection questions, you are supporting this work. Here is a list of questions to get the reflection process started:

- What did you learn from this work?
- What are you proud of in this piece?
- What would you have done differently?
- What was the most challenging part?
- How could you improve this work?
- How did other people help you finish this work?
- How will doing your best on this assignment help you in the future?

Pan Balance

Have students hold out their arms on both sides of their bodies. Ask them a reflection question that has two possible answers. Students should respond by tipping one arm lower than the other (as if one side of the scale is heavier). Here are some example questions:

- Did you talk too much or too little?
- Were you distracted or engaged?
- Did you rush or take too much time?
- Did you stay calm or get angry?
- Was your response safe or unsafe?

Calibrating Student Assessments

Supporting student self-assessment means calibrating their thinking. You will have students who make mistakes but evaluate themselves as though they have never made a mistake in their lives. At the other end of the spectrum, you will likely see students who will be too hard on themselves. In both these cases, having a periodic calibration can help to support accuracy in their evaluations. The *Calibrating Student Assessments* chart is provided in the Digital Resources (calibrating.pdf).

Teaching Assessment

In addition to assessing students, consider the effectiveness of your own instruction. The *Teaching Rubric* can be found in the Digital Resources (teachingrubric.pdf). Use this tool to evaluate your SEL instruction. You may wish to complete this rubric at different points throughout the year to track your progress.

Skills Alignment

Each activity in this book is aligned to a CASEL competency. Within each competency, students will learn a variety of skills. Here are some of the important skills students will practice during the year.

 Self-Awareness

Identifying Emotions

Personal and Social Identities

Cultural and Linguistic Assets

Honesty

Identifying Personal Strengths

Developing Interests

Values

Understanding Emotions

Examining Biases

 Self-Management

Managing Emotions

Personal Agency

Helping Others

Self-Discipline

Organizational Skills

Self-Motivation

Stress Management

Setting Goals

Planning

Self-Monitoring

 Social Awareness

Taking Others' Perspectives

Helping Others

Empathy

Gratitude

Integrity

Identifying Social Norms

Compassion

Recognizing Others' Strengths

Social Norms

Skills Alignment *(cont.)*

Relationship Skills	
Making Friends	Resisting Peer Pressure
Resolving Conflicts	Teamwork
Positive Relationships	Nonverbal Communication
Leadership	Seeking Help
Effective Communication	Cultural Differences
Standing Up for Others	

Responsible Decision-Making	
Identifying Solutions	Critical Thinking
Curiosity	Making Reasoned Judgements
Solving Problems	Anticipating Consequences
Considering Options	Evaluating Consequences

Setting the Stage for Kindergarten

Kindergarten is a special and unique grade. Compare two kindergartners, and you will find that nearly nothing is the same about them. Some are ready to learn letters and sounds. Others are already reading.

This book was written with that difference in mind. Depending on the student, text on the page may need to be read aloud. Directions may need to be read to students, especially early in the year. As the year progresses, students may be able to read the text more independently.

Additionally, some pages include short stories which may also need to be read to students. Consider the listening comprehension and attention span of your students as you determine how much text to read at a time. You may want to have students complete a task prior to going on to the next story.

Tasks on each page are primarily drawing. Support students with written tasks using these ideas:

- Have students write simple sentences using sentence frames. For example: I feel _____.
- Create a bank of words students can use to complete sentence frames or for independent writing.
- Use a highlighter to write words or sentences on students' papers that can be traced.

Ideas on most pages can be extended in the following ways:

- Encourage students to write their own sentences related to their drawings.
- Guide a discussion related to the topic.
- Allow time for students to share their drawings and ideas with partners or with the whole group. Discuss similarities and differences of ideas.
- Connect SEL ideas to books read aloud or other content areas.
- Encourage students to practice SEL ideas throughout the day.

It is important to remember that activities for social-emotional learning are most effective when combined with adult-led conversations. These conversations can help students as they develop SEL skills to cope with the world. Your guidance will set the tone for the activities each day.

How You Feel

School may be a new place. You will have a lot of feelings about it.

Directions: Draw what your face looked like the night before school. Draw what it looked like on your way to school. Draw what it will look like after school.

night before school

on your way to school

after school

Adult Directions: Discuss how students felt before school and how they might feel after school. Talk about what those emotions would look like.

Name: _____ Date: _____

How You Feel

It can be hard to sit still. You can move just one part of your body.

Directions: Try each action. Circle one that feels good to you.

shoulder circles

finger presses

slow breathing

head rolls

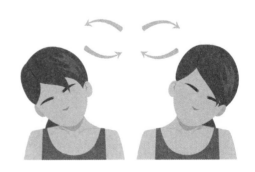

Name: _____ Date: _____

How Other People Feel

People do not all feel the same. You can look at their faces. That can show how people are feeling.

Directions: Circle the happy face in yellow. Circle the sad face in blue. Circle the mad face in orange. Circle the nervous face in green.

- -

Adult Directions: Help students identify what the different emotions mean and how they feel.

Name: _____ Date: _____

Make New Friends

It is fun to find new friends. You can make a friend by doing things together.

Directions: Draw one thing you can do with a friend.

Focus on Self

Relationship Skills

Name: _____ Date: _____

Take a Break

Learning can make you tired. You may need to take a break. There are many ways to let your brain rest.

Directions: Color the break you like the most.

Name: _____ Date: _____

126956—180 Days of Social-Emotional Learning

Focus on Family

Self-Awareness

Your Family Is Special

You are part of a family. It is not like other families. That is a good thing.

Directions: Draw your family. Circle yourself in the drawing.

Adult Directions: Write the word *family* on the board, and define it. Discuss the ways in which families can be similar and different.

Name: _____ Date: _____

Be a Helper

You can do jobs at home. Jobs help your family.

Directions: Circle how you can help. Draw one more job you can do.

Name: _____ Date: _____

How to Help

Do you know when your family needs help? Look for ways you can help

Directions: Circle how you know the person needs help. Draw how to help.

- -

Adult Directions: Before students draw, help them brainstorm a list of ways to help the person in the picture.

Name: _____ Date: _____

Learn to Share

Families share a lot. It is nice to share. But it can also be hard.

Directions: You can share toys. Draw two ways to share a ball.

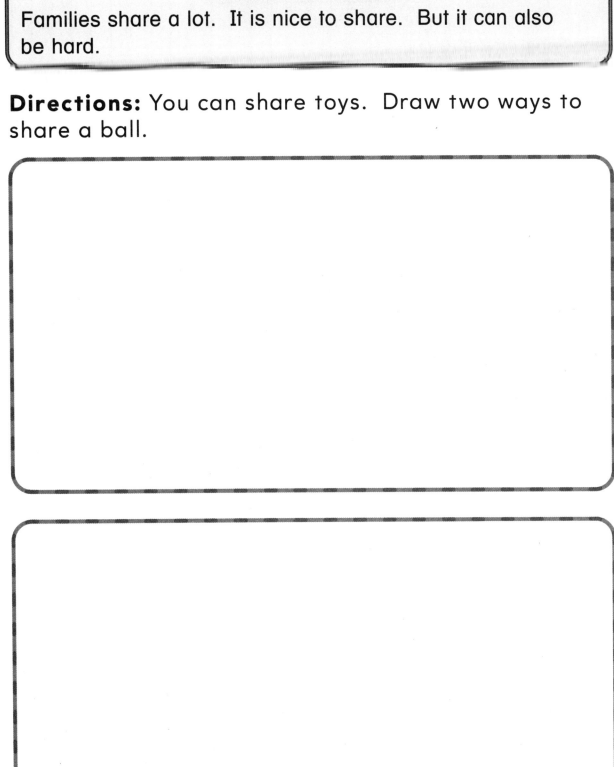

Name: _____ Date: _____

Help Your Family

You can help your family. You can share jobs. This makes the jobs easier.

Directions: Look at the pictures. Circle things that would help. Write an **X** on things that would not help. Draw one more thing you could do to help your family.

Fight with your sister.

Help your grandparent.

Do not put things away.

Clean your room.

Name: _____ Date: _____

How to Start Talking

You can make new friends. You may not know what to talk about. Start by talking about you.

Directions: Draw each of your favorite things. Tell a new friend about your drawings.

My Favorite Color

My Favorite Food

My Favorite Thing to Do at Home

My Favorite Thing to Do at School

- -

Adult Directions: Read the four categories students will draw. Provide suggestions if needed.

Name: _____ Date: _____

Meeting New People

It can be hard to talk to a new person. It is okay to feel shy. Smile and say hello. Make a new friend.

Focus on Friends

Self-Management

Directions: Draw a friendly face. Trace the word *Hello*.

Hello

© Shell Education

Other People's Feelings

Think about your friends' feelings. This makes you a good friend.

Directions: Read the stories. Draw how Raj feels after each one.

Raj's cat is lost. Raj and his dad looked for it. They cannot find his cat. How does Raj feel?

Raj is eating dinner with his family. They hear a noise. They look and see his cat by the door. How does Raj feel?

Focus on Friends
Social Awareness

Name: _____ Date: _____

Strong Friendships

You can make a new friend by doing things you both like.

Directions: Circle the things you like to do. Draw your favorite thing to do with a friend.

biking

reading

sports

pretend play

art

Be Curious

There are new friends all around you. Look for a kid you do not know. Smile at them. Talk to them. Then, you can make a friend.

Directions: Think of how to make a new friend. Write a number on each line to show the right order. Color the pictures.

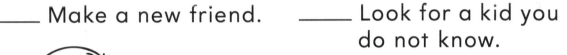

_____

_____ Make a new friend.

_____ Look for a kid you do not know.

_____

_____ Smile at the person.

_____ Talk with the person.

Hello!

- -

Adult Directions: Discuss the four steps to making a new friend before students attempt to order the process on their own.

Name: _____ Date: _____

How You See Yourself

You are super! Think about what makes you feel good about yourself.

Directions: Draw your favorite things.

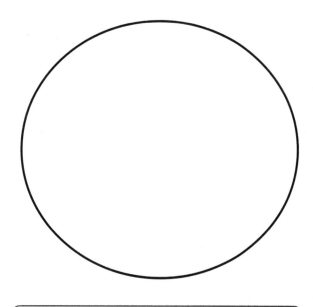

| my favorite animal |

| my favorite book |

| my favorite fruit |

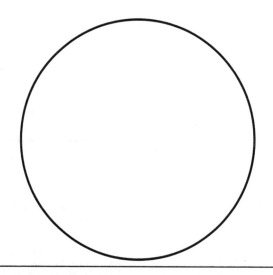

| my favorite activity |

Name: _____ Date: _____

Emotions Show-and-Tell

It feels good to show how we feel. It also feels good to tell others what we like.

Directions: Draw one thing that makes you feel good. Then, draw one thing you like to do.

I feel good when I...

I like to...

Name: _____ Date: _____

Focus on Self

Social Awareness

Kind Words

People will tell you when you do a good thing. They may thank you. Kind words can feel like a warm hug.

Directions: Read the kind words. Draw a face to show how they would make you feel.

Thank you!

You were great!

You did a good job!

You worked so hard!

Name: _____ Date: _____

Fun with Friends

Others may be good at the same things as you. It is fun to do those things with them.

Directions: Circle the things you do well. Talk to a partner. Learn what they are good at. Draw a star by the things you both do well.

| reading |

| sports |

| art |

| building |

Name: _____ Date: _____

Focus on Self

Responsible Decision-Making

New Skills

It is fun to learn a new skill. It helps to set a goal. Then, practice. This will help you learn.

Directions: Draw what you would like to learn. Write an **X** each day you practice.

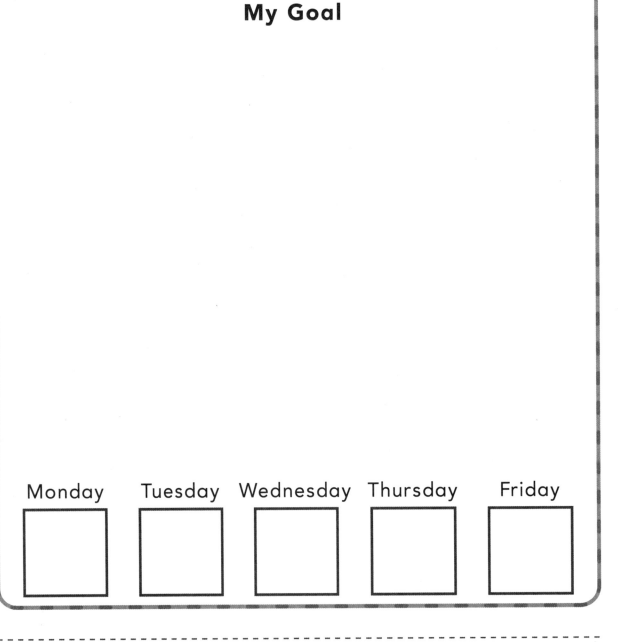

My Goal

Monday	Tuesday	Wednesday	Thursday	Friday
☐	☐	☐	☐	☐

Adult Directions: Model this activity by making a group goal together and charting its progress.

Name: _____ Date: _____

Your Neighborhood

Your neighborhood is where you live. The places in it make it special.

Directions: Draw your neighborhood. Draw the things that make it special.

- -

Adult Directions: Talk with students about their various neighborhoods. Discuss how they are similar and different.

Name: _____ Date: _____

Focus on Neighborhood

Self-Management

The People near You

You can help people who live near you. You can say nice things. You can do nice things too.

Directions: Make a plan to help a neighbor.

_____

_ _

1. I will help: _____

2. Draw how you will help.

3. Draw how you will both feel.

Do the Right Thing

There may be a lot of kids near you. Kids might play without adults. Kids still need to do the right thing.

Directions: Read the stories. Draw the right thing to do.

Abdi is at the park for the first time. Abdi wears clothes that are different from the other kids. Some kids tease Abdi about his clothes. Some kids tease him about his name.

There are flowers growing in a neighborhood garden. Some kids walk in the garden. They step on the plants. The kids pull up the plants and throw them at each other.

Name: _____ Date: _____

Be a Leader

Most groups have leaders. A leader should say nice things. A leader should do the right thing.

Focus on Neighborhood

Relationship Skills

Directions: Circle the leaders doing the right thing. Write an *X* on leaders doing the wrong thing.

Let everyone have a turn!

We don't want to play with you.

You can't play with us!

You can play with us.

Make Choices

You may play with a lot of kids in your neighborhood. It can be hard to choose what to do. You can take turns.

Directions: Look at the games. Circle your favorite. Talk to a friend about a game you both want to play. Color that game.

Name: _____ Date: _____

Students at School

Kids at school are students. Students learn. Students play. Students make new friends.

Directions: Color the letters. Draw one thing a student does.

STUDENT

Always Do Your Best

There might be things you do not want to do at school. You still need to do them. Remember, it is your job. You should do your best. You will feel good when you do.

Directions: Draw how your face looks when you do your best.

I will do my best!

Focus on School

Self-Management

Name: _____ Date: _____

Rules at School

Places have their own rules. There are rules at school that you may not have at home. There are rules at home that you may not have at school.

Focus on School

Social Awareness

Directions: Circle school rules in red. Circle home rules in blue. Draw another rule. Have a friend guess if it is for home or school.

Clean up dishes.

Walk in a line.

Raise your hand.

Put clean clothes away.

My Rule

Name: _____ Date: _____

How to Listen

You need to listen at school. When you listen, you will learn a lot. Look at the person who is talking. Keep your hands still. Think about what you hear.

Directions: Look at each body part. Draw a line to match what it should do when you listen.

Look.

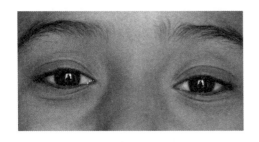

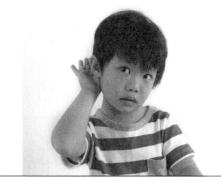

Listen.

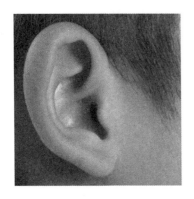

Be still.

Focus on School

Relationship Skills

Name: _____ Date: _____

School Helpers

Many people work at a school. They are there to help you.

Directions: Draw the helpers at your school. Tell a friend what the helpers do.

teacher	nurse
librarian	cafeteria worker
principal	custodian

Adult Directions: Before students start to draw, discuss what these helpers do. Tell them the names of these helpers in their school. Work together to list all the things these helpers do.

Name: _____ Date: _____

Have Fun

Think about what you like to do. When you do things you like, you will feel good.

Directions: Draw the best part of your day. Make sure your face matches how you feel.

Name: _____ Date: _____

Get Excited

It feels good to be excited. That means you are really happy.

Directions: Think of a time you were excited. How did you act? Color the picture that shows what you did.

run

shout

smile

cheer

Adult Directions: Talk more with students about the definition of *excited*. Share examples, and have them generate their own ideas before they color.

Be a Helper

Sometimes, friends have bad days. You can help.

Directions: Read the stories. Draw how you can help.

The class is playing. Malik is alone.

Rowa is trying to read. The book is too hard.

Name: _____ Date: _____

Lift Others Up

We feel good when we help others. We can make hard jobs easier. We can tell them what they do well.

Focus on Self

Relationship Skills

Directions: Color one thing a friend does well. Then, tell them about it.

reading

math

running

art

Name: _____ Date:_____

Try New Things

Doing something well can make you feel good. That can help you when you try a new thing.

Directions: Color the words. Then, draw something you want to try.

I can do it!

Name: _____ Date: _____

Celebrate Special Days

Some days are special. There are holidays. There are other days too. How do you celebrate?

Directions: Think about a day you celebrate. Draw what you do.

Things to Think About

What do you wear?   Who else is there?

What do you eat?   What do you do?

Where do you go?   What makes you excited?

Adult Directions: Read "Things to Think About" aloud. As students consider a celebration to draw, talk about possible holidays and other observed days (such as Martin Luther King Jr. Day) and what it means to celebrate them.

Focus on Family | Self-Awareness

Name: _____ Date: _____

Holiday Countdown

It is fun to celebrate. It is hard to wait for those special days.

Directions: Color each number. Count down to a special day. Write what you will celebrate.

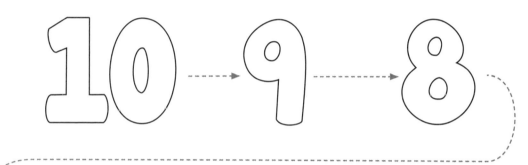

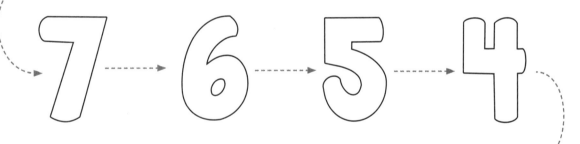

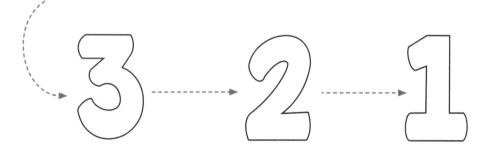

_____

- - - - - - - - - - - - - - - - - - - -

Time to celebrate _____ !

- -

Adult Directions: Before students color the countdown, have them brainstorm the holidays or special days they celebrate. Write the list for students to see. Then, have them write a holiday or celebration on the line.

Name: _____ Date: _____

The Joy of Gifts

Celebrations are fun. You may get a gift. You can make gifts for others. Gifts make you feel good.

Directions: Draw a gift someone gave you. Draw a gift you could make. Write who you would make it for.

A Gift Someone Gave Me

I would make a gift for _____.

126956—180 Days of Social-Emotional Learning   © Shell Education

Name: _____ Date: _____

Special Words

Some special days have special words. We say them to each other. It is a nice thing to do. It is a way to celebrate.

Directions: Say the words. Color the words you use.

Holee Mubaarak!

Happy Hanukkah!

Happy Thanksgiving!

Happy Diwali!

Happy Juneteenth Day!

Merry Christmas!

Happy Birthday!

¡Feliz Día de los Muertos!

- -

Adult Directions: Read the greetings aloud. Explain the holidays they represent (Feliz Día de los Muertos means "Happy Day of the Dead" in Spanish. Holee Mubaarak means "Happy Holi" in Hindi.) Allow students to share any other greetings they use.

Name: _____ Date: _____

Deciding What to Wear

It is good to wear the right thing. Knowing where you are going can help you choose what to wear.

Focus on Family

Responsible Decision-Making

Directions: Read the stories. Draw what you would wear.

You are going to a wedding. All your family will be there. Friends will be there too. It will be fancy. What will you wear?

You are going to a birthday party. It is a pool party. You will get to swim. You will have lunch and cake. What will you wear?

Name: _____ Date: _____

Be Honest

You should tell your friends things that are true. This makes you feel good. It makes you a good friend too.

Directions: Read the stories. Circle how each friend feels.

1. Allen tells his friend he likes their shoes.

2. Lucy tells her friend that she does not like her shirt.

3. Mike tells his friend that he will not play with him.

4. Audrey tells her friend that she wants to play together.

5. Greg tells his friend that they are good at baseball.

Name: _____ Date: _____

Focus on Friends

Self-Management

Help Your Friends

Friends help each other. It is good to ask if a friend wants help first.

Directions: Color the words. Practice saying them. Draw yourself helping a friend.

Can I help you?

Name: _____ Date: _____

Your Friends' Feelings

It is good to think about how your friends feel. You can help if they feel bad.

Directions: Read the stories. Draw how you could help.

> Your friend built a tall block tower. Someone bumped into it. The tower fell down. Your friend is sad.

> Your friend is crying. Your friend tells you their stomach hurts.

Name: _____ Date: _____

Focus on Friends

Relationship Skills

Be Nice

You might see someone who is not being nice. It is okay to tell them to be nice. Or you can find an adult.

Directions: Trace the words. They will show you how to help.

Be nice!

Tell an adult.

Name: _____ Date: _____

Plan Ahead

It is good to make plans with friends. It helps to think about what you both like.

Directions: Write things you and your friend can do. Circle what you will do the next time you see your friend.

1. A game we can play is...

_____

_____

2. A toy we can use is...

_____

_____

3. A snack we can eat is...

_____

_____

Adult Directions: Help students generate lists for each category. Write ideas where students can see them. Help students write their own ideas, as needed.

Name: _____ Date: _____

Focus on Self
Self-Awareness

Things You Do Well

Sometimes, things are hard. You may feel upset. There are things you can do. You can think about what you do well.

Directions: Think of one thing you do well. Draw yourself thinking about that thing.

Name: _____ Date: _____

You Can Do Hard Things

You learn when you try things that are hard. Having a plan can help you do hard things.

Directions: Write **1** by what you will do first. Write **2** by what you will do next. Write **3** by what you will do last.

_____
_____ Try to do it on my own.

_____
_____ Listen to the teacher.

_____
_____ Ask for help.

Name: _____ Date: _____

Helpers Are All around You

Lots of people can help you. Helpers are all around you.

Directions: Read the stories. Draw who could help you.

Your tooth was loose all day. Now, it is in your hand!

You are in the library. You can't find a book.

Name: _____ Date: _____

Ask for Help

Hard times can make you want to hide. It is better to find some help.

Directions: Color the words. Use these words when you need help.

Focus on Self

Relationship Skills

Name: _____ Date: _____

Solve Problems

Some problems you can solve on your own. Some need an adult's help.

Directions: Do you need an adult? Can you fix it yourself? Place a ✓ in the right box.

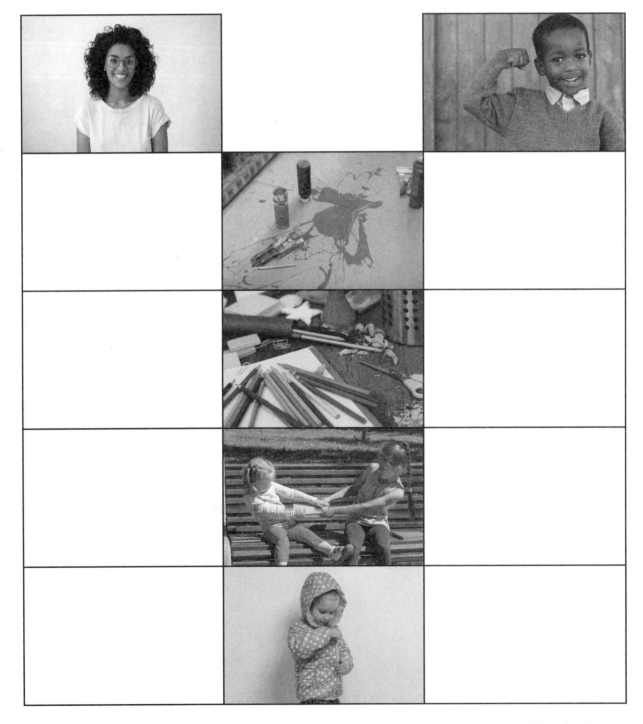

Be Honest

When we tell the truth, we are honest. That means we do not lie. We tell all that we know.

Directions: Draw a time when you were honest. Draw a time when you were not honest.

Honest

Not Honest

Name: _____ Date: _____

How to Calm Down

It can be hard to be honest when you are worried. You may be afraid of what is next. It is good to stop and think. Take some breaths. Count to five.

Directions: Trace each number. Practice taking breaths. Count while you are doing it. Then, draw how you feel.

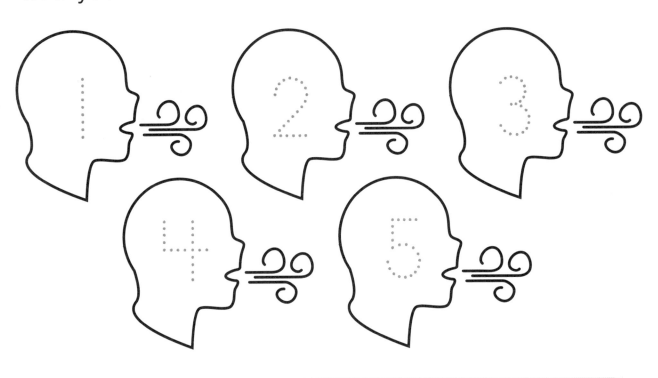

Name: _____ Date: _____

Always Be Honest

There are times when other people will not be honest. But you still need to tell the truth. This can be hard to do.

Directions: Read the story. Answer the questions.

You are playing ball with your friend Juan. He throws the ball. It hits his mom's car. It leaves a dent. Later, his mom sees it. She asks what happened. Juan says he does not know.

1. How does Juan feel? Draw his face.

2. How does Juan's mom feel? Draw her face.

3. Draw what you would do.

Name: _____ Date: _____

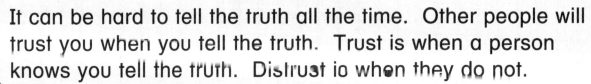

Tell No Lies

It can be hard to tell the truth all the time. Other people will trust you when you tell the truth. Trust is when a person knows you tell the truth. Distrust is when they do not.

Focus on Neighborhood

Relationship skills

Directions: Write a word from the Word Bank on each line. Then, draw a person you trust.

distrust	trust

1. What happens when you tell the truth?

_____

- -

_____

2. What happens when you tell a lie?

_____

- -

_____

Think Before You Act

We all make choices. We think about how to act. We think about a lot of things when we make choices. We decide if it is a good choice.

Directions: Read the two endings to the story. Circle the choice you would make.

Story: You are at your neighbor Mary's house. Her mom is baking cookies. She says you can have some if you ate lunch. You did not eat lunch. But you really want a cookie. What do you do next?

Choice 1	Choice 2
Say you have eaten lunch.	Say you have not eaten lunch.
You get a cookie.	Maria's mom gives you lunch instead of a cookie.
You feel happy to get a cookie. You feel bad you were not honest.	You feel bad you do not get a cookie. You feel happy you were honest.

- -

Adult Directions: Read aloud the story and choices. Have students color the boxes as you read each one. Compare and contrast the two choices and their outcomes before students circle their choices.

Name: _____ Date: _____

Focus on School

Self-Awareness

Me at Home and School

You know a lot about yourself. Others may not know as much about you. Friends at school may not know how you are at home.

Directions: Draw what you do well at home. Draw what you do well at school.

Home

School

- -

Adult Directions: Lead a discussion about whether friends at school know about students' home lives and whether families know about students' lives at school.

Name: _____ Date: _____

Rules

We have to work with others when we are at school. We do this to get along. We do it so things go smoothly. It is why there are rules at school.

Directions: Draw a rule that is hard for you to follow at school. Draw how you can do better.

A Hard Rule

How I Can Do Better

Name: _____ Date: _____

Home and School Are Different

School and home are not the same. There are a lot more people at school.

Focus on School

Social Awareness

Directions: Draw what you would do at home. Draw what you would do at school.

1. cleaning up

Home	School

2. telling an adult something

Home	School

3. eating lunch

Home	School

Teams Really Work

You work with other students at school. You may not agree on how to do things. So, you will have to find ways to work as a team.

Directions: Read the story. Draw two ways you could solve the problem.

Your teacher reads a book. She gives you a sheet of paper. She gives your friend some crayons. She asks you to work as a team to draw about the book. You and your friend do not agree about what to draw.

Way 1

Way 2

Focus on School

Relationship Skills

Name: _____ Date: _____

Learning from Others

There are a lot of students at your school. You can notice things about them. This will help you learn new things from them.

Directions: Draw one thing you learned from a friend. Draw one thing you want to learn from someone at school.

Something I Learned

Something I Want to Learn

Name: _____ Date: _____

You Are Special

You are a special person. No one is just like you. Thinking about that can help you feel good.

Directions: Draw at least three things that make you special.

Focus on Self

Self-Awareness

Name: _____ Date: _____

Breathe through Feelings

You can have big feelings. Taking slow, deep breaths can help. They can make your feelings seem smaller.

Directions: Take some deep breaths. Draw how you feel in the big balloon. Color the other balloons.

Adult Directions: Have students imagine blowing up balloons. Have them take deep breaths in, put their lips together, and pretend to blow air into balloons. Have students repeat this five times. Then, have them complete the activities on the page.

Other People's Feelings

People act in many ways. Think about how a person feels. It may help you understand.

Directions: Read each story. Draw how each person feels.

Jonas is crying. His lunch tray is on the floor by his feet.

Hannah is in art class. She has a big smile on her face.

Focus on Self

Social Awareness

Name: _____ Date: _____

Focus on Self

Relationship Skills

Tell How You Feel

You can tell people how you feel. You can do it without words.

Directions: Try each way to talk without words. Practice with a partner. Talk about what each action means. Color the one you like best.

A Big Smile

A Wink

A Head Nod

A Wave

Name: _____ Date: _____

Help Solve Problems

You may see a person with a problem. You can help. It feels good to help others.

Directions: Look at the problems. Draw a line to the way you can help.

Problems	Ways to Help

Name: _____ Date: _____

How to Say Hello

Families talk to each other a lot. They use language to talk.

Focus on Family

Self-Awareness

Directions: Tell your family how you say hello. Learn a new way. Try the new way with your family. Draw you and your family talking.

Adult Directions: Take a dictation, and write what the student says in the speech bubbles.

Be Brave

You may not see some of your family a lot. It can be hard to talk to them. You may not know what to say. Try talking about you!

Directions: Draw each item. Tell a friend about the things you like.

My Favorite Food	My Favorite Game

My Favorite Show	My Favorite Toy

Focus on Family

Self-Management

Name: _____ Date: _____

Language

We use a lot of words to talk. Together, they are our language. Not all people speak the same language.

Directions: Imagine you hear a language you do not know. Color the box that says what you may think. Then, draw how you would feel.

That language sounds like my language.	That language does not sound like my language.
I want to learn that language.	I want to know what they are saying.

Adult Directions: Read the four options in the boxes aloud. Talk about the feelings associated with each.

Talk without Words

You can tell people things using words. Or you can use no words. Your body can show how you feel. Your face can show it too.

Directions: Circle the word that shows how each person is feeling.

1.

sleepy   excited

2.

worried   happy

3.

bored   glad

4.

calm   cheerful

Adult Directions: Explain what each emotion word means before students begin the activity.

Name: _____ Date: _____

You Can Help

A lot of people use English. But not all people. Some parents do not speak English. Their kids can help them.

Directions: Read the story. Draw a picture to go with it.

Lena's aunt speaks Spanish. She does not speak English. She wants to order food. The server only speaks English. Lena speaks English and Spanish. She can help her aunt. She can tell her what the server says. She can tell the server what her aunt says.

Name: _____ Date: _____

Help a Friend

People all around you need help. When you work with a friend, you can help more. It can be a lot of fun to help with a friend!

Directions: Circle the job you would like to do with a friend. Draw you and your friend doing the job.

raking leaves

picking up trash

shoveling snow

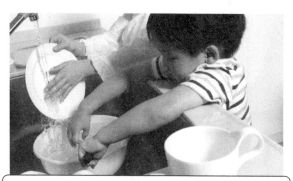

washing dishes

Name: _____ Date: _____

Try New Things

It can be hard to try new things. Being with a friend when you try can help you feel better.

Focus on Friends

Self-Management

Directions: Read the stories. Draw how you would feel.

Today is the first day of swim lessons. You get to the pool, and don't see anyone you know. A few minutes before the class starts, your friend walks in. You go stand by your friend. Draw how you feel.

Your big brother takes you to the park to play. There are a lot of big kids there. You look at the swings and see your friend. You walk over and swing with your friend. Draw how you feel.

Name: _____ Date: _____

Cheer with Friends

Sometimes, your friends feel sad. You can help cheer them up.

Directions: A note can cheer someone up. Write a note. Give the note to someone who may be sad. Use the Word Bank to help.

Word Bank	
Feel better!	You did a great job!
I like you!	You are special!

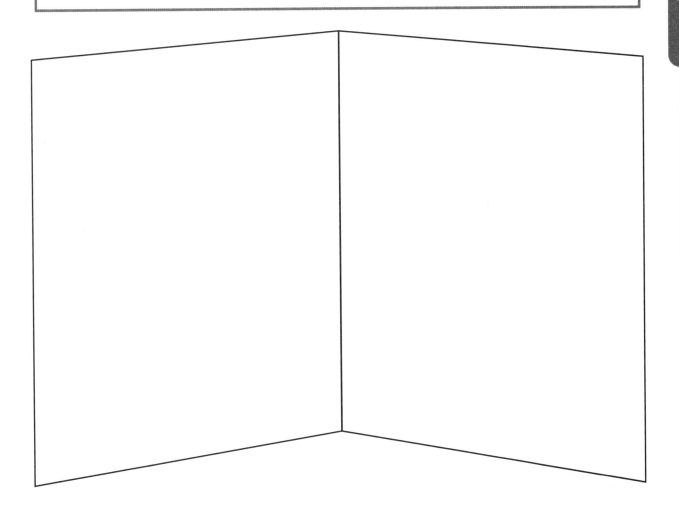

- -

Adult Directions: Help students use the Word Bank for writing, if needed.

Name: _____ Date: _____

A Team of Friends

You can work with a friend on a project. You will get more done. You will become better friends too.

Directions: Build a block tower by yourself. Write the number of blocks you used. Build a block tower with a friend. Write the number of blocks you used. Circle the bigger number.

1. When I built a tower on my own, I used _____ blocks.

2. When I worked with a friend, we used _____ blocks.

Adult Directions: Provide blocks for stacking.

Name: _____ Date: _____

Choices with Friends

Friends can help you make good choices. You can talk to a friend and decide the right thing to do.

Directions: Read the stories. Write or draw to show the right thing to do.

Someone who is not nice to you lost their pen. You know where the pen is.

_____

_ _

_____

You see two students on the playground. They are yelling. One is pushing the other.

_____

_ _

_____

Name: _____ Date: _____

Listen to Your Body

Your body knows how you feel. It is good to think about how you feel. Your body can give you a sign.

Directions: Draw a line from each feeling to how it makes your body feel.

happy

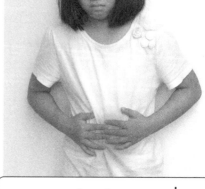

upset stomach

angry

ready to move

nervous

tense

Name: _____ Date: _____

Make a Plan

It is easy to get excited. It can be hard to wait. It can help to make a calendar. You can mark off days. You can see when a special day is coming.

Directions: Write the dates. Circle the day of a fun event. Cross off each day. Soon, you will be at the day with the circle.

Sunday	Monday	Tuesday	Wednesday	Thursday	Friday	Saturday

- -

Adult Directions: Help students add numbers to the calendar. Then, help them find and circle the day of a fun event.

Name: _____ Date: _____

Focus on Self

Social Awareness

Other People's Stories

People can act in a lot of ways. Think about how other people feel.

Directions: Read the stories. Circle the person's feeling.

It is time to leave school. Jess cannot find her backpack.

mad   happy   sad   worried

Levi's mom comes to school on his birthday. She has a wrapped book for the class.

excited   angry   happy   embarrassed

Name: _____ Date: _____

Your Face and Your Feelings

Our faces show how we feel. This means people can see our feelings

Directions: Circle one feeling. Draw how your face looks when you feel that way.

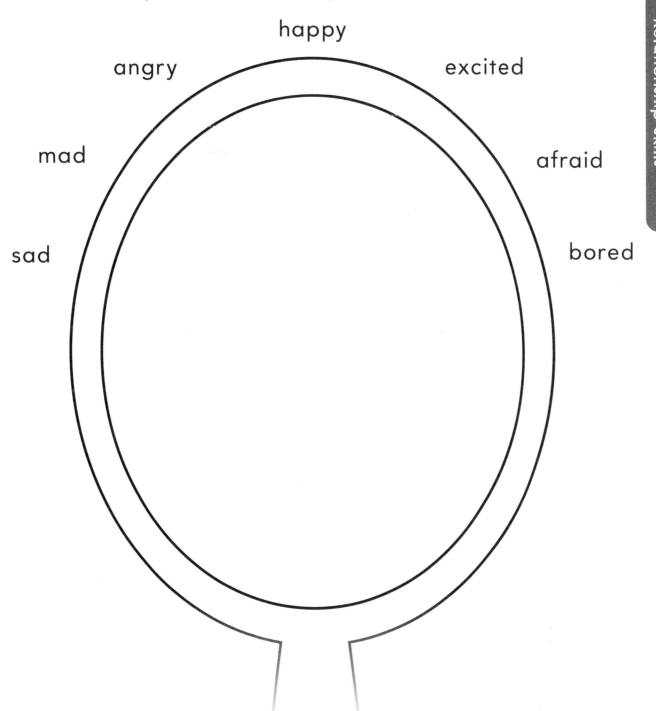

happy

angry   excited

mad   afraid

sad   bored

Name: _____ Date: _____

Act Your Best

There are a lot of ways you can act. Some are better than others.

Directions: Read the stories. Draw the best way to act.

Your library book is missing. What should you do?

Your birthday is here. The party is about to start. How should you act?

Name: _____ Date: _____

Thank the People Who Help You

A lot of people in your neighborhood are nice. They may help you. They look out for you. They say nice things. It is good to thank these people.

Directions: Think of three neighbors who help you. Write their names above the snowflakes. Color the snowflakes. Thank your neighbors for helping you.

_____   _____

_____   _____

_____

_____

Focus on Neighborhood

Self-Awareness

Adult Directions: Help students write names above the snowflakes.

Name: _____ Date: _____

Plan to Say Thank You

A goal is something you try to do. People set goals. You can set a goal to show a neighbor you are thankful. It helps to make a plan.

Directions: Write the name of a kind neighbor. Draw your neighbor being kind. Draw your plan to say thank you. _____

My neighbor is _____ .

How My Neighbor Is Kind

How I Will Say Thank You

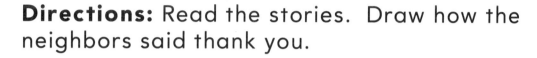

Ways to Say Thank You

If you do a nice thing for a neighbor, they might thank you. There are many ways to say thank you. You can say thank you with words. You can say thank you with a smile. You can say thank you with a small gift. You can say thank you by helping.

Directions: Read the stories. Draw how the neighbors said thank you.

It is winter. There was a big snow storm. Jack shoveled his neighbor's walk. Jack's neighbor brought him cookies and a thank you note.

Sophie's neighbor got a dog. Then, her neighbor hurt his foot. Sophie takes the dog for walks. Sophie's neighbor smiles and waves to Sophie.

Focus on Neighborhood

Social Awareness

Name: _____ Date: _____

Focus on Neighborhood

Relationship Skills

Fun with Neighbors

It is fun to do things with neighbors. It helps to know what you like doing. Then, you can see if others want to do it too.

Directions: Write or draw things you like to do with neighbors. Circle one you can do today.

Outside Games	Inside Games

Name: _____ Date: _____

Help Neighbors with Problems

Neighbors will have problems. You can help. It takes just a few steps.

Directions: Read the steps to solve a problem. Draw each step. Try this next time there is a problem with a friend in your neighborhood.

1. Talk about the problem.	
2. Think about your feelings.	
3. Find a solution.	

Focus on Neighborhood

Responsible Decision-Making

- -

Adult Directions: Read and discuss problem-solving steps.

Name: _____ Date: _____

Big, Medium, and Small Feelings

Our feelings can be big. Or they can be small. We might feel happy. We might feel really happy. It is good to think about all our feelings.

Directions: Circle a feeling word. Draw to show yourself when it is a small, a medium, and a big feeling.

Feelings		
happy	sad	mad

Small Feeling	Medium Feeling	Big Feeling

 126956—180 Days of Social-Emotional Learning

Name: _____ Date: _____

Celebrate Hard Things

Sometimes, things at school are hard. You might not like those hard things. It can help to think of a fun thing to do when you are done.

Directions: Draw one thing that is hard at school. Draw one fun thing to do when it is done.

This Is Hard For Me

This Will Be Fun

Focus on School

Self-Management

Name: _____ Date: _____

A Hard Day's Help

You might see a friend having a hard day. You can help your friend. Think of what help you would need. You can do more than you might think!

Directions: Draw what you need on a hard day. Draw how you can help a friend on a hard day.

On a hard day, I need...

When my friend has a hard day, I can...

Focus on School

Social Awareness

Stop and Check

You might think a friend is being mean. But you might not have understood what your friend said. It can help to stop and check. Stop and ask questions. Check to see if you heard what they tried to say.

Directions: Put the pictures in the right order. Write a number by each one.

_____

_____

_____

Name: _____ Date: _____

Compromise

There are a lot of ways to solve problems. You can tell people what to do. Or you can each give a little. This is called a *compromise*.

Directions: Read each story. Then, draw how the friends could compromise.

Joel and Lauren are outside. Lauren wants to build a snowman. Joel wants to go sledding.

Alma and Eric are at the art center. They both want to paint. There is only one space for painting.

Adult Directions: Discuss examples of compromise before students begin drawing.

Emoji Talk

We can use pictures to talk to each other. We may use emojis. They show how we feel.

Directions: Draw lines to match the feelings to the faces. Then, draw your own emoji.

Feelings

1. happy

2. loving

3. sleepy

4. surprised

5. sad

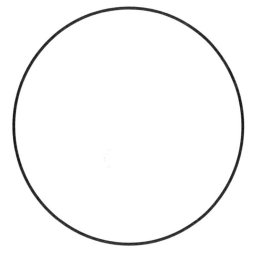

Focus on Self
Self-Awareness

Name: _____ Date: _____

Too Much Technology

Technology is a lot of fun. It can be easy to spend too much time with it. It is good to take a break. It can help if you have other things to do.

Directions: Draw the ways to spend less time with technology. Circle the one that is best for you.

Set a Timer	Play a Board Game
Go Outside	**Find a Friend**

Name: _____ Date: _____

Safe Spaces

You need to be safe in a lot of places. Follow all the rules to stay safe.

Directions: Draw a 🏠 if it is a rule in your life. Draw a 💻 if it is a rule for the internet. Draw both if the rule is for both places.

Rule	Drawing
1. Don't talk to strangers.	
2. Keep your password a secret.	
3. Get help if something does not seem right.	
4. Don't tell people who you don't know where you live.	
5. Be kind.	
6. Don't open a message if you don't know who it is from.	

Name: _____ Date: _____

Giving and Finding Help

Sometimes, people need help. You can try to help them.
Sometimes, you will need help. You can ask for help.

Directions: Read the stories. Then, draw what you can do next.

You are working on a laptop. Your screen goes black. You are not sure what happened.

Your friend is drawing a picture on a tablet. She does not know how to make a neat circle. You know how to use the circle tool.

Name: _____ Date: _____

Internet Safety

Things can happen when you use technology. You have to know what to do to be safe.

Directions: Read the stories. Draw a ★ next to the things that are okay to click. Write an **X** next to the things you should not click.

1. You are watching a video. A funny looking box pops up. It looks like you can click on it. You do not know what it is for.

2. You are playing a game on the internet. The game stops. A continue box pops up.

3. You are playing a game online. A box pops up. It wants you to type your name.

4. You are on a website you have been on before. A parent helped you make a password. The password box pops up.

- -

Directions: Draw an adult who can help you decide what is okay to click.

Name: _____ Date: _____

Try New Things

We do things our families like to do. It is fun to do those things. It is also fun to try new things.

Directions: Draw one thing you like to do with your family. Draw a new thing you would like to try.

Focus on Family

Self-Awareness

Something I Like to Do with My Family

A New Thing I Would Like to Try

Name: _____ Date: _____

Follow the Example

People in your family do things well. They may do them better than you. You can react in a lot of ways. You do not need to feel bad.

Focus on Family

Self-Management

Directions: Read the stories. Circle what you should do.

1. You hear your brother playing the piano. He can play a very hard song. You wish you could play too.

Get mad.   Ask to take lessons.

2. You are tossing a football to your grandpa. He knows how to throw the ball straight. You throw the ball sideways.

Practice throwing   Run in the house
the ball.   and hide.

3. You and your sister are building block towers. Your sister's is very tall. Yours is small.

Kick over your   Ask your sister
sister's blocks.   for help.

Name: _____ Date: _____

Focus on Family

Social Awareness

Compliments

You can say a nice thing to someone. Tell them they did a good job. This is a compliment.

Directions: Write a compliment for each person.

1. Your brother plays the piano. He plays hard songs.

   You are really good at

   _____

   — — — — — — — — — — — — — — — — — —

   _____.

2. Your grandpa knows how to throw a football straight. He can throw it far too.

   You are really good at

   _____

   — — — — — — — — — — — — — — — — — —

   _____.

3. Your sister is using blocks. She is building a tower. It is as tall as she is.

   You are really good at

   _____

   — — — — — — — — — — — — — — — — — —

   _____.

Adult Directions: If needed, circle a word that students could write.

Name: _____ Date: _____

Be a Team

Working as a team can get jobs done. We can learn from others. We can work faster.

Directions: Plan a family dinner. Write who will do each job. Circle a job you can learn how to do.

Job	Person
Make the dinner.	
Set the table.	
Clear the table.	
Wash the dishes.	
Clean the counter.	

Name: _____ Date: _____

Focus on Family

Responsible Decision-Making

Help through Self-Talk

You may not want to try new things. You may be afraid. You may not know what to do. Self-talk can help. Self-talk is what you say to yourself.

Directions: Read the self-talk steps. Then, draw yourself trying a new thing.

Step 1	Step 2	Step 3
Look at what you need to do. Think about the best way to do it.	Ask for help if you need it.	Be positive.
Self-Talk: What do I need to do?	**Self-Talk:** Who can help me?	**Self-Talk:** I will try my best. I will work hard.

Adult Directions: Read each step aloud. Discuss how to use self-talk with student examples.

Name: _____ Date: _____

Work Hard to Be Kind

A good friend is kind. Being a kind friend is the right thing to do.

Directions: Read the story. Write or draw how you can be kind.

You have been sad. Your friend was playing with someone else. Later, you see your friend all alone. Your friend looks sad.

_____

_____

_____

_____

Focus on Friends

Self-Awareness

Name: _____ Date: _____

Focus on Friends

Self-Management

Think Before You Speak

You have many feelings. You can share how you feel with your friends. But it is good to think about what you say.

Directions: Think about what you want to say to a friend. Finish each sentence. Then, draw each one.

_____

_ _ _ _ _ _ _ _ _ _ _ _ _ _ _ _ _ _

1. I like it when you _____.

2. I wish you would _____.

Showing Thanks to Friends

It is good to let friends know you care. You can tell them why you are glad they are your friends. This is being thankful.

Directions: Draw one of your friends. Write your friend a note to say thank you.

Name: _____ Date: _____

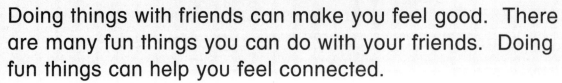

Connect with Friends

Doing things with friends can make you feel good. There are many fun things you can do with your friends. Doing fun things can help you feel connected.

Directions: Draw yourself on one puzzle piece. Draw your friend on the other puzzle piece. Show what you like to do together. Then, finish the sentence.

My friend and I feel connected when we

_____

_____.

Show Your Heart

It feels good to do nice things. Others think good things about me when I do nice things.

Directions: Read the words. Draw something nice you have done. Write two of the words in the hearts.

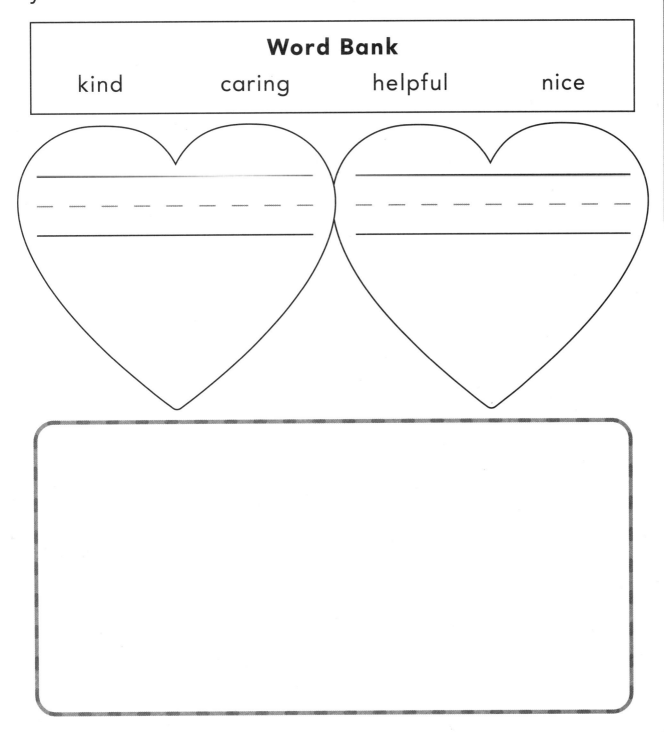

Word Bank

kind   caring   helpful   nice

Focus on Friends

Responsible Decision-Making

Name: _____ Date: _____

The Names of Anger

Anger is a strong feeling. It is okay to feel angry. Anger can have a lot of names.

Directions: Draw a time you felt each kind of anger.

1. mad—upset	**3. jealous**—wanting what someone else has
2. irritated—something is bothering you	**4. frustrated**—something is hard

Adult Directions: Discuss examples of each emotion before students begin drawing.

Name: _____ Date: _____

You and Your Anger

It is not fun to feel angry. There are a lot of things you can do when you feel angry.

Directions: Read the story. Draw one thing that would help. Draw one thing that would not help. Draw a star by what you would do.

You want to play with your friends. You don't want to play the game they pick. You feel yourself getting angry.
What would help?
What would not help?

- -

Adult Directions: For the first box, prompt students to draw things such as suggesting another game, playing with someone else, or finding the fun in this game. For the second box, prompt students to draw more impulsive reactions.

© Shell Education   126956—180 Days of Social-Emotional Learning

Name: _____ Date: _____

Focus on Self

Social Awareness

Everybody Gets Angry

You can see when others feel angry. They might tell you they are angry. Their bodies can tell you too.

Directions: Look at the picture. Circle how you know the boy is angry. Circle the kind of anger he might be feeling.

mad   frustrated   irritated   jealous

Name: _____ Date: _____

Steps to Solve a Problem

You may make other people angry. You may not know they are angry. You can try to help.

Directions: Think about the steps to solve a problem. Trace the dotted lines to show each step. Then, read the story. Tell someone how you would solve the problem.

Ask what the problem is.

Brainstorm ideas.

Choose the best one.

Do it.

You are playing blocks with a friend. You get a good idea. You want to use only blue blocks. You gather them together in a pile. Your friend starts to yell. He starts to cry. He starts to clench his fists too. Practice the four steps.

- -

Adult Directions: Read aloud the problem-solving steps.

Name: _____ Date: _____

Calming Down

Other people know when you are angry. They can feel it. You show it. But you can calm down. That makes other people feel better. It makes you feel better too.

Directions: Draw what your face looks like for each feeling. Think about how someone who is with you would feel. Draw their face.

1. I am angry.

2. I am calm.

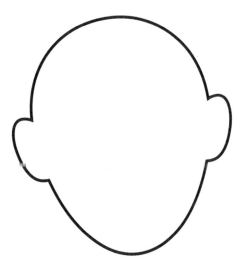 

Adult Directions: Discuss how students' feelings affect others.

Name: _____ Date: _____

Watch Your Feelings Grow

Feelings can grow. They can start small. They can become big and strong. Anger is a feeling that can grow very fast.

Directions: Read the ways to be mad. Draw a time you felt each way.

1. irritated—something bothers you

2. angry—you are very upset

3. furious—you are very, very angry

Name: _____ Date: _____

Help with Anger

You can be a little mad. You can be furious. Anger can grow fast.

Focus on Neighborhood **Self-Management**

Directions: Read the story. Write the feeling you would have for each part. Use the Word Bank to help you.

Word Bank

irritated—something bothers you

angry—you are very upset

mad—you are upset

furious—you are very, very angry

Your neighbor does not have a bike. You let him borrow yours.

1. He leaves it outside. He does not lock it up.

_____

_____

2. He borrows it again. This time, he keeps it at his home.

_____

_____

Name: _____ Date: _____

Help Others Calm Down

You can notice when others are mad. You can help them calm down.

Directions: Read the story. Draw how you could help your neighbor calm down.

Your neighbor is trying to ride a bike. She falls over. She does not want to try anymore. She is very mad. She starts to cry.

Name: _____ Date: _____

Focus on Neighborhood

Relationship Skills

Active Listening

You can learn to listen. This will help you to be a good neighbor. Being a good listener is a skill. It is called *active listening*.

Directions: Read how to be an active listener. Draw each step.

Look at the person.	Draw two eyes.
Listen to what they say.	Draw two ears.
Check if you understood. Say what the person said in your own words.	Draw the other person.
Say something to calm things down.	Draw a speech bubble.

 126956—180 Days of Social-Emotional Learning

Name: _____ Date: _____

Stop and Reflect

To reflect is to think about an event. What went well?
What could you do next time?

Directions: Read the story. Reflect on what happened. Write or draw what June could do next time.

June is playing with her neighbor Amil. Amil hands June one of his sister's toys and tells her to pull it. They both start tugging on the toy in a tug-of-war. Amil's sister sees what they are doing. She yells for them to stop. Amil tells June his sister is a crybaby and not to worry about her. June is almost winning. She keeps pulling on the toy. Soon, the toy breaks in two pieces. Amil's sister screams loudly.

Name: _____ Date: _____

An Arm's Length Away

Some people are close to us. We keep other people farther away. This is called an *arm's length*. This can keep us safe.

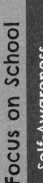

Directions: Who are you close to? Write their names in the inside circle. Who do you stay an arm's length from? Write their names in the outside circle.

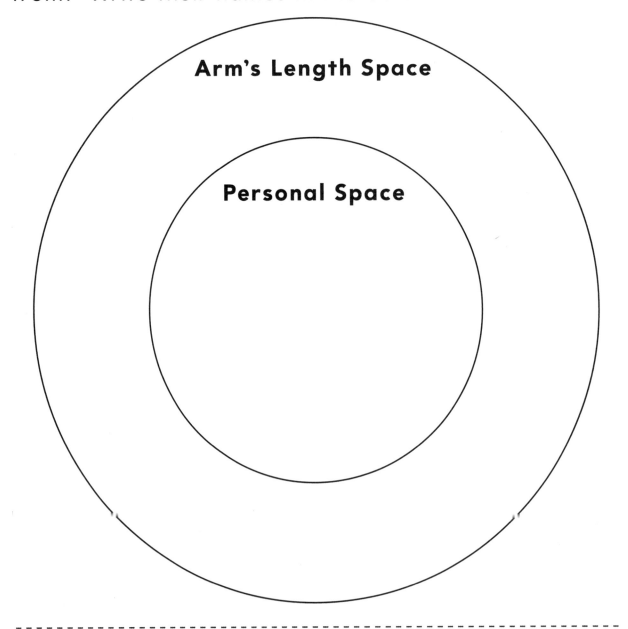

Arm's Length Space

Personal Space

- -

Adult Directions: Elaborate on personal space and arm's length space so students understand the difference.

Name: _____ Date: _____

Don't Get Too Close

Some people like to be very close. Other people like a lot of room. It is good to know how you feel. It is good to see how others feel too.

Directions: Read the story. Draw two things you could do.

Chris is in your class. He loves to be around people. He stands very close to you all the time. Sometimes, he touches your arm. You do not like to be so close. You do not want him to touch you. What could you do?

Focus on School

Self-Management

Name: _____ Date: _____

Close Enough

You are with other people a lot of the time. You may need to be close. You may need to be far away. It is good to know how close you should be.

Directions: Read the stories. Circle how close you should be for each one.

1. You are with a partner. You are sharing a book.

very close   close   arm's length

2. You are with a friend. You are building with blocks.

very close   close   arm's length

3. You go to your teacher's desk. You ask her a question.

very close   close   arm's length

4. A friend is sad. She asks for a hug.

very close   close   arm's length

5. You are in line to go to lunch.

very close   close   arm's length

You Get to Choose

You can use your space in different ways. You choose who can come close. You choose who stays farther away. It is always your choice.

Directions: Write the name of a person who you let do each action.

1. hold hands: _____

2. shake hands: _____

3. stand a few feet away: _____

4. hug: _____

5. put me on their lap: _____

6. stand close to: _____

Adult Directions: Discuss the types of relationships. Talk about why it is okay to be closer to some people than others. Reinforce that these are students' decisions.

Name: _____ Date: _____

Focus on School

Responsible Decision-Making

Fix Your Problems

Some problems are small. You can solve them by yourself. Other problems are big. You will need an adult's help to solve them.

Directions: Read the stories. Draw what you can do.

You are standing in line. The child in front of you turns around and screams in your face.

You love to play handball at recess. You play with Gabe and he loses. He gets very close to you. He yells about all the reasons he thinks he didn't lose.

Name: _____ Date: _____

Find Your Happy Place

Being happy feels good. There are a lot of ways to be happy.

Directions: Draw a line to match the feeling to the picture. Then, draw a time you were happy.

loving—liking a person or a thing a lot

hopeful—wishing something will happen

interested—being curious

confident—knowing you can do something

- -

Adult Directions: Read aloud each feeling and definition. Have students share about times they were happy.

Name: _____ Date: _____

Focus on Self
Self-Management

Find Confidence

Believing in yourself can make you happy. This is called *confidence*. It can take a long time to feel this way.

Directions: Use red to color the skills you are confident in. Use blue to color the skills you could do better.

riding a bike

reading

playing a sport

doing math problems

tying shoes

playing an instrument

Directions: Choose one skill you colored blue. Draw what you can do to practice on another sheet of paper.

126956—180 Days of Social-Emotional Learning

Name: _____ Date: _____

Be Thankful

We all have things to be thankful for. Being thankful can make you happy.

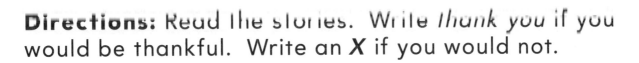

Directions: Read the stories. Write *thank you* if you would be thankful. Write an **X** if you would not.

1. You need to take out the trash. Your sister helps you.

_____

- -

_____

2. You want to pick a movie. Your brother picks before you can.

_____

- -

_____

3. A family friend comes to visit. He brings a gift for you.

_____

- -

_____

4. Your aunt takes you and your brother to the park.

_____

- -

_____

Adult Directions: Read the stories to students as needed.

Name: _____ Date: _____

Things in Common

People have many things they like to do. We can do those things with our friends. Doing things with friends makes us happy. These are things we have in common.

Directions: Think of someone who likes each thing. Write their names on the lines. Draw a star next to the things you like too.

_____

- - - - - - - - - - - - - - - - -

_____

_____

- - - - - - - - - - - - - - - - -

_____

_____

- - - - - - - - - - - - - - - - -

_____

_____

- - - - - - - - - - - - - - - - -

_____

Curious and Happy

Being curious is a good thing. It can help you learn new things. And learning new things can make you happy!

Directions: Circle one thing you are curious about. Learn more about it. Draw one new thing you learned.

an animal—the pangolin   **a country**—Nepal

a sport—disc golf   **a person**—C. J. Walker

a food—ramen   **a thing**—a geyser

Adult Directions: Read aloud the choices, and provide a basic explanation of each. Help students research the chosen items with books and videos.

Name: _____ Date: _____

Focus on Family

Self-Awareness

Your Values

Values are the things that are most important to you. They help you live your life. They shape your actions. Your family teaches you a lot of values. You show your values by the way you live.

Directions: Read the values in the boxes. Color three that mean the most to you. Draw how you feel when you show one of your values.

responsibility	gratitude

fairness	helpfulness

kindness	

honesty	

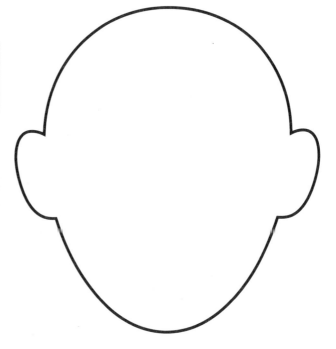

Adult Directions: Explain each of the values to students. Define them, and provide examples.

Name: _____ Date: _____

Being Organized

Being helpful is a value. It is good to help your family. A chart can help.

Directions: Write a ✓ to show how you help your family. Draw a ★ to show how you could start helping.

Name: _____ Date: _____

Give Gratitude

Being thankful is a value. It is called *gratitude*. You can say thank you to your family.

Directions: Trace thank you. Color the picture. Say thank you to someone today.

© Shell Education

Resolving Conflicts

Words can hurt your family's feelings. You can say things to make it better. That is called an *apology*.

Directions: Read the steps of an apology. Color each step. Use the steps when you need to.

1. Go to the family member.

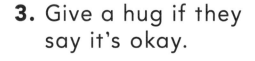

2. Say, "I'm sorry."

3. Give a hug if they say it's okay.

Name: _____ Date: _____

Stop, Think, Choose

You should try to make good choices. It is good for your family when you make good choices. You can stop and think. You can think about what to do next.

Directions: Read the story. Stop and think. Draw a good choice you could make. Draw a bad choice. Circle the one you would do.

You are playing ball in the house. The ball hits a lamp. The lamp falls and breaks. What are two choices you can make?

Good Choice	Bad Choice

Name: _____ Date: _____

Don't Judge by Looks

How people act means more than how they look. Choose friends who do good things. It does not matter what they look like.

Directions: Read the stories. Write what each person is like. Use the Word Bank.

Focus on Friends
Self-Awareness

Word Bank	
helpful	polite
mean	selfish
nice	unkind

Doug has nice shoes. His shirts are always cool. Doug grabs toys from other students. He pushes them down. He throws sand. What is Doug like?

_____

_ _

_____

Zoey's hair is messy. Her shirt is often dirty. Zoey helped a person at the store. She put their cart away. She picked up a box that was on the floor. What is Zoey like?

_____

_ _

_____

Adult Directions: Help students use the Word Bank to write descriptive words.

Name: _____ Date: _____

Focus on Friends

Self-Management

How to Be Upset

One day, you will be upset with a friend. Be careful how you act when you are upset. It is okay to take a break. It is okay to say you are not happy. Be nice when you talk.

Directions: Trace and say the words. Then, draw pictures to match the words.

I need a break.	That made me upset.
I didn't like that.	Please don't do that.

Face Their Feelings

The way a friend looks can show how they feel. Look at a friend's face. Think about their feelings. Why do you think they feel that way?

Directions: Look at each face. Use the Feeling Words to write how the person feels.

Focus on Friends
Social Awareness

Feeling Words		
sad	angry	excited

1. This person feels

_____

_ _ _ _ _ _ _ _ _ _ _ _ _ _

_____.

2. This person feels

_____

_ _ _ _ _ _ _ _ _ _ _ _ _ _

_____.

3. This person feels

_____

_ _ _ _ _ _ _ _ _ _ _ _ _ _

_____.

Adult Directions: Help students use the word bank, if needed.

Name: _____ Date: _____

Steps to Fix a Problem

You can fix a problem with a friend. There are steps to help. When you follow the steps, it can make things better.

Directions: Read the story. Talk about each step to fix the problem with a partner.

Ben and Sam were playing catch at the park. Ben kept throwing the ball over Sam's head. Sam had to run and get the ball every time. Sam fell and hurt his knee when he ran for the ball. Sam threw the ball back hard. The ball hit Ben's leg. Ben and Sam are both mad.

Steps to Fix Problems

1. What is the problem?

2. Think of how to solve the problem.

3. Choose the best idea.

4. Try it.

5. Did it work?

Have Fun Alone

You do not need to play with the same friend all the time. You can play with other people. Or you can play on your own.

Directions: Write two things you can do by yourself. Draw each one.

I can _____ .

I can _____ .

Name: _____ Date: _____

Focus on Self

Self-Awareness

Surprise!

Surprise is a big feeling. There are a lot of ways to be surprised.

Directions: Read each kind of surprised feeling. Draw a time you felt that way.

excited—ready for something to happen	**confused**—mixed-up or not understanding
amazed—filled with wonder	**eager**—wanting very much

Set Small Goals

You may want to do something well. This takes time. It takes practice too. Setting goals can help you practice. Set smaller goals to help you reach the end goal.

Directions: Draw something you want to do well. Draw two small goals that would help along the way. Follow the example.

Focus on Self

Self-Management

First Small Goal	Second Small Goal	End Goal

Name: _____ Date: _____

Focus on Self

Social Awareness

See People's Feelings

You can see how other people feel. You can show concern. You can be happy for them too.

Directions: Read what the feelings mean. Then, read the stories. Write how each person feels. Use the feelings words.

amazed—filled with wonder

confused—mixed-up or not understanding

excited—very ready for something to happen

1. A package comes to your house. Your parent did not order it.

   _____

   _

   _____

2. Your brother loves space. He sees a planet in the night sky.

   _____

   _

   _____

3. Your friend's grandma is coming for a visit. Your friend has not seen her for a long time.

   _____

   _

   _____

Name: _____ Date: _____

Don't Be Confused

It does not feel good when you do not understand. This is called *being confused*. But you can get help.

Directions: Read the stories. Write who could help.

Helpers			
brother	dentist	librarian	teacher

1. You are learning something new in math. You don't understand what to do.

_____

_ _ _ _ _ _ _ _ _ _ _ _ _ _ _ _ _ _

_____

2. You want to check out a book. You do not know how to find it in the library.

_____

_ _ _ _ _ _ _ _ _ _ _ _ _ _ _ _ _ _

_____

3. You do not know how to level-up in a video game your family plays.

_____

_ _ _ _ _ _ _ _ _ _ _ _ _ _ _ _ _ _

_____

4. You need to brush your molars better. You do not know what a molar is.

_____

_ _ _ _ _ _ _ _ _ _ _ _ _ _ _ _ _ _

_____

Relationship Skills

Focus on Self

Name: _____ Date: _____

Focus on Self

Responsible Decision-Making

Check Your Mindset

We need to be willing to try new things. When we do, we might feel amazed! This is called a *growth mindset*. The opposite is a *fixed mindset*. That is when you do not think you can do it.

Directions: Read each sentence. Put a ✓ by each growth mindset. Write an **X** by each fixed mindset.

☐ I can do hard things.

☐ I will try to get better.

☐ I give up.

☐ This is too hard.

☐ I can learn how to do this.

☐ I will do my best.

☐ I will try another way.

☐ I am going to make a mistake.

Directions: Draw how you feel when you have each mindset.

Growth Mindset	Fixed Mindset

Name: _____ Date: _____

Always Tell the Truth

Friends will get into trouble. It is best to tell the truth. You will feel better when you say what is true.

Directions: Read the stories. Circle what the people should say.

Ethan, Mica, and Chris are playing with Ethan's bike at the park. Ethan has to go home. He lets Mica and Chris keep playing with his bike. He tells them to give it to him later. Mica and Chris forget. They leave his bike at the park. What should Mica and Chris say?

A big kid took the bike and ran away with it.

We are sorry. We left the bike at the park.

Jon and Amy are playing tag. They do not watch where they go. They run through their neighbor's garden. They smash and break plants. The garden does not look nice. What should Jon and Amy say?

We are sorry. We ran in your garden.

We saw a bunny in your garden. We wanted to get closer.

Name: _____ Date: _____

Make Group Goals

A neighbor may need help. Neighbors can help each other.
It is good to plan how to help.

Directions: Read the story. Make a plan to help
by putting the actions in order. Then, draw the
people helping.

Mr. Withers was in a car accident. He has a cast
on his leg. He has a hard time taking care of his
yard. His neighbors want to help him.

_____ Neighbors sign up to do jobs.

_____ Neighbors talk and decide to help.

_____ Neighbors take turns doing jobs.

_____ Neighbors make a list of jobs to do
for Mr. Withers.

Name: _____ Date: _____

Different Rules

You have rules at your home. Your neighbors have rules at their homes. Some rules are the same. Some rules are different. It is good to follow the rules at a neighbor's home.

Directions: Draw or write two rules you have at your home. Draw or write two rules at your neighbor's home. Draw a star next to rules that are the same.

Rules at My Home	Rules at My Neighbor's Home

Focus on Neighborhood
Social Awareness

Name: _____ Date: _____

You Can Say No

People may try to make you do things. You might not want to do those things. It is okay to do what you want to do. It might be hard, but you can say no. You are brave when you do this.

Directions: Read the story. Write and draw the brave thing to do.

Andy took his sisters to the park. Two of Andy's friends saw them there. They asked Andy to go to the pool. Andy knows his sisters need him at the park. Andy thinks his friends won't like him if he says no. What should Andy do to be brave?

_____

_____

_____

_____

_____

Name: _____ Date: _____

Fixing Problems

There are times neighbors do not get along. It is normal to have problems with friends. You can learn what caused the problems. You can work to fix the problems. You can still be friends.

Focus on Neighborhood

Responsible Decision-Making

Directions: Read the story. Answer the questions.

Joy, Luz, and Tim want to make money to help a neighbor. They want to have a lemonade stand. They each want the stand to be at their house. They have a fight about where to put it. They all go home mad.

1. What caused the problem?

_____

_____

_____

_____

_____

2. How can the problem be fixed?

_____

_____

_____

_____

_____

Name: _____ Date: _____

Rain, Rain, It's Okay

Rainy days at school can be hard. You do not get to play outside. Other plans may change too. You can still have fun and learn on a rainy day.

Directions: What things can you do on a rainy day? Draw them on the umbrella. Who will you play with? Write their names under the umbrella.

Focus on School

Self-Awareness

Name: _____ Date: _____

Trying New Things

There are always new things to try. It can be hard to try something new. But trying new things can be good for you.

Directions: Draw yourself trying the new things.

A New Food	A New Book
A Different Way to Solve a Math Problem	**Playing with a New Friend**

Focus on School

Self-Management

Name: _____ Date: _____

Other Points of View

People see the same event in different ways. The way you see things is your point of view. Try to think of how other people see things. Think of their points of view.

Directions: Read the stories. Draw each point of view. Tell a partner how each person is feeling.

Kari had a hard morning. She woke up late. She spilled her breakfast. She missed the bus. When she got to school, she would not smile at her friend.

1. What is Kari's point of view?

Dave brought his brother's ball to school. He lost the ball at recess. Dave is worried his brother will be mad. When Dave's brother asked to read a book with him, he yelled "No!"

2. What is Dave's point of view?

Name: _____ Date: _____

Teams Can Work

It is good to know how to work with others. You can do more work. You can have more fun. Working with other people is called *teamwork*.

Directions: Plan a class garden. Color the steps. Write a friend's name by each job.

bring dirt and seeds

_____

- - - - - - - - - - - - - - - - -

_____

plant seeds

_____

- - - - - - - - - - - - - - - - -

_____

bring pots

_____

- - - - - - - - - - - - - -

_____

water plants

_____

- - - - - - - - - - - - - -

_____

Name: _____ Date: _____

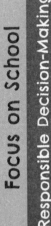

Focus on School

Responsible Decision-Making

Your School Needs You

You can help at your school. This will make your school a better place. When you help, others are thankful. When you help, you feel good.

Directions: Circle one way you can help at school. Draw and write how you will feel when you help.

_____

_____

_____

_____

Name: _____ Date: _____

Name Your Feelings

Fear is a strong feeling. It can make you feel a lot of ways. Things are not as scary when you know what to call your feelings.

Directions: Read the stories. Use the Feelings Words to write how you would feel.

Focus on Self
Self-Awareness

Feelings Words

embarrassed—feeling foolish

scared—afraid

worried—concerned about what might happen

1. You drop your lunch tray. Food and milk spill everywhere.

_____

- - - - - - - - - - - - - - - - -

_____

2. Your brother wants you to go on a roller coaster with him. You have never been on one. You hear people screaming. It is very tall.

_____

- - - - - - - - - - - - - - - - -

_____

3. Your sister is going on a trip. She will be gone for three nights. You have never been away from her for a whole night.

_____

- - - - - - - - - - - - - - - - -

_____

Name: _____ Date: _____

Focus on Self

Self-Management

Things You Can't Control

Bad things will happen to you. Sometimes, you can control those things. You can make them better. Other times, you have no control. There is nothing you can do. But you can learn how to react to those things. It is good to know the difference. It is good to know what to do.

Directions: Color in blue the things you can control. Color in red the things you cannot control. Draw how the red boxes make you feel.

who my friends are	how people treat me
the words people say	the way I act
the words I use	my attitude
the choices I make	the choices other people make

© Shell Education

Feeling Humiliated

Things may happen that make you feel embarrassed. Other people will feel this way too. You can try to help. That can make them feel better. It can make you happy too.

Directions: Read the story. Draw how you can help.

Sam is excited to go play. He runs across the grass. He does not see a muddy patch. He slips and falls in the mud. Other kids see him fall. They start to point and laugh.

Social Awareness

Focus on Self

Name: _____ Date: _____

Focus on Self

Relationship Skills

What Other People Think

We all want to feel included. It makes us feel good. So, you may be afraid of what others think of you. People may say things about you that are not nice. Stop and think about what is true. That will make you feel better.

Directions: A classmate named Mara shows off her new shoes. She looks at your shoes and says, "Those are dirty." Circle how you would react.

Ignore

Don't let what Mara said bother you. Walk away.

Use Humor

Tell Mara that dirty shoes make you run faster.

Say Something Nice

Tell Mara that her shoes look pretty.

- -

Directions: Draw a time when you were afraid of what others thought of you.

Feeling Worried

Your body knows when you are worried. You can feel it.
You can help your body feel better. You can make good
choices.

Directions: Use red to color how your body shows It
is worried. Use blue to color the ways to feel better.

Responsible Decision-Making

Focus on Self

Picture a stop sign in your head.	Count to 10.
Your stomach feels like it has butterflies in it.	Ask for help.
Your head hurts.	Hug a stuffed animal.
Think of a happy thought.	Draw a picture.
Your hands are sweaty.	Take a walk.

Name: _____ Date: _____

Every Family Is Different

The things you do are normal to you. But other families do other things. They may seem strange to you. They are normal to them. We are all different. That is a good thing.

Directions: Draw to answer each question. Share your answers with a friend. Circle the things that are different.

1. How do you greet an older person?

2. Where do you put your shoes when you come home?

3. What is your family's favorite food?

Name: _____ Date: _____

I-Messages

People may say mean things to you. They may hurt your feelings. You can tell the person how you feel. You can use I-messages.

Directions: Think of a time someone made you feel sad. Draw what happened. Then, finish the I-message to show your feelings.

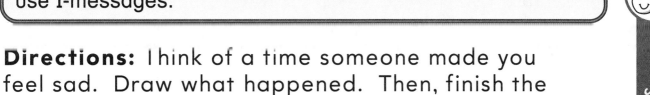

Self-Management

Focus on Family

_____

I feel _____

_____

when you _____.

Adult Directions: Model a few I-messages before students create their own.

Name: _____ Date: _____

Focus on Family

Social Awareness

Learn from Other Families

Families are not all the same. Be careful what you say. You do not want to hurt feelings. Stop and listen. You can learn new things.

Directions: Read each story. Circle what you would do.

1. Your friend is eating lunch. The food looks different from the food at your house.

   Tell them the food looks weird.   Ask what they are eating.

2. You go to your friend's house. You see a large pile of shoes outside the door.

   Wear your shoes.   Take off your shoes.

3. Your friend was not at school yesterday. It was a holiday you have never heard of.

   Ask your friend about the holiday.   Tell your friend that it is not a real holiday.

Your Culture

Culture is the way a family lives. It is how we celebrate. It is how we speak. It is the food we eat. It is the clothes we wear. It is the music we listen to. It is so much more.

Directions: Circle one item from your culture. Draw what your family does. Draw what another family does.

Focus on Family
Relationship Skills

Culture Items

food	custom	language
clothing	holiday	music

My Family

Another Family

Name: _____ Date: _____

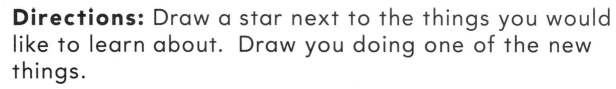

Learn from Other Cultures

You can try things from other cultures. They may be different. But you might like them.

Directions: Draw a star next to the things you would like to learn about. Draw you doing one of the new things.

1. May 5 is Children's Day in Japan. Families fly flags. They are shaped like fish. Each fish stands for a person in the family.

2. People in China slurp their soup. They do it to show the soup is good.

3. Sinterklass is a Dutch holiday. People write poems about family.

- -

Adult Directions: Read the text aloud. Explain more about each holiday or custom, as needed.

Name: _____ Date: _____

Check with a Friend

You might think you do something well. A friend might think you could get even better. It is good to think about how you are as a friend. Then, check in with a friend. See if they agree.

Focus on Friends

Self-Awareness

Directions: Circle three words from the Word Bank that describe you. Ask a friend if they agree with your words.

Word Bank		
excited	funny	listener
friendly	helpful	patient

Directions: Draw you and your friends.

Adult Directions: Explain what each word in the Word Bank means.

Name: _____ Date: _____

Focus on Friends

Self-Management

Make a Friend Plan

You might not see your friends as much as you would like. It can help to make a plan to see a friend. Your family can help you.

Directions: Draw what you want to do with your friend. Then, write your friend's name. Write what you want to do with them.

My friend is _____.

I want to _____ with my friend.

Name: _____ Date: _____

You Can Help Your Friends

A friend might have a hard time. You can be a good friend and be concerned. You can think about what is wrong. You can help them feel better.

Directions: Read the stories. Draw how you can help each person feel better.

1. Lauren's family is going on a trip. This will be Lauren's first time on an airplane. Lauren is nervous.

2. Calvin is going to play soccer. He is on a new team. He does not know anyone on the team. The coach is new too.

Name: _____ Date: _____

The Power of Friends

Friends feel good when we tell them why we like them.
Take time to think about why a friend is special. Tell your
friend what you like about them.

Focus on Friends

Relationship Skills

Directions: Draw a friend. Write about that friend.

_____

My friend's name is _____.

I like to _____ with my friend.

My friend is great at _____.

Name: _____ Date: _____

Being Curious

Summer is a good time to try new things. You can do things with a friend. Think of all the new things you have done. You are ready to do more things!

Directions: Think of one new thing to try. Write who you will try it with. Draw both of you doing this new thing.

I will try  _____.

I will do this with

_____.

Name: _____ Date: _____

Types of Sad

There are a lot of ways to feel sad. Sometimes, you can get over it quickly. Other times, it takes longer.

Directions: Color the box red if you would be a little sad. Color the box blue if you would be very sad.

Your brother is going to camp. He will be gone a whole week.	Your parents told you to clean your room. You forgot. They are upset.
Your grandma is sick. You are not able to see her.	You want to play outside. It is raining.

Directions: Draw a time you were sad.

Focus on Self

Self-Awareness

Focus on self

Self-Management

WEEK 34
DAY
2

Name: _____ Date: _____

Get Back to Happy

It is okay to be sad. But it does not feel good to stay sad for too long. You can find things to make you feel happy again.

Directions: Draw a thing that makes you sad. Draw what could make you happy again.

I'm sad when...

I'm happy when...

© Shell Education 126956—180 Days of Social-Emotional Learning 179

Name: _____ Date: _____

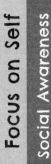

Focus on Self

Social Awareness

When Others Feel Lonely

Feeling lonely is a sad feeling. You can see when others feel lonely. You can help them. You can be their friend.

Directions: Circle how you know the girl feels lonely. Draw how to help her.

Beat Boredom

It does not feel good to be bored. But you can find ways to have fun. Having people around you can help. You can do things with those people.

Directions: Draw what you look like when you are bored. Then, circle all the things you would like to do with a friend.

Focus on Self

Relationship Skills

Things to Do

play a board game   go to the park

play a sport   make up a play

do a craft   create a dance

go on a nature walk   ride a bike

Name: _____ Date: _____

The Power of Words

Be careful what you say. The things you say can make people feel good or bad. Your words can make things happen.

Directions: Read the story. Draw two ways Jamal could react. Circle the best way.

Jamal wants to go to the park. His friends want to play a board game. Jamal does not want to play the game. He gets very upset.

Way One

Way Two

Different Customs

People do not all live the same way. Some neighbors do things that are different. This is not wrong. We can learn a lot from other people.

Directions: Read each item. Write **yes** if you do it. Write **no** if you do not do it.

1. Do you listen to special music for holidays?

_____

2. Do you go to a place of worship?

_____

3. Do you burn incense in the house?

_____

4. Do you speak a different language at home than at school?

_____

5. Do you have special clothes for holidays?

_____

6. Do you take your shoes off before you go in the house?

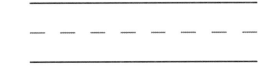

Focus on Neighborhood

Self-Awareness

Neighbors Are Teachers

Your neighbors may do things differently than you. But that is okay. You can learn from them.

Directions: Read the stories. Write questions you could ask to learn more.

1. Your neighbor is decorating his home. He says it is for a holiday. You have never heard of the holiday before.

   _____

   -

   _____

   _____

   -

   _____

2. You are at a picnic. You start to eat right away. Your friend waits for an adult to eat first.

   _____

   -

   _____

   _____

   -

   _____

Choose Your Words

Your words can make people happy. Or they can make people sad. It is good to think about other people. That can help you choose the right words.

Directions: Read the stories. Color the face that shows how your neighbor would feel for each story.

1. You are playing outside with a neighbor. It is close to dinner. There is a strong smell from your neighbor's house. It is a new smell to you. You tell your neighbor it is stinky.

2. It is not winter. Your neighbor puts lights on their house. You put lights on your house in the winter. You say, "Can you tell me about your lights? They're so pretty!"

3. Your neighbor is going to a party. She is dressed up. The clothes do not look like clothes you wear. You ask why she is wearing a Halloween costume.

Name: _____ Date: _____

Stand Up for Neighbors

You can help other people. You can speak up if you see things that are wrong. You can make things better.

Directions: Read the story. Write what you would say to make things better. Then, draw what you would do.

You are outside with friends. Your friend's mom comes out to talk to him. They speak a language you do not know. His mom goes back inside. Another friend pretends to speak the language. Everyone starts to laugh. Your friend looks very sad.

_____

- -

_____

_____

- -

_____

Learn from Your Neighbors

You can learn a lot from people in your neighborhood. They can teach you new things. You may learn a new thing to do.

Directions: Think about a neighbor who could teach you something new. Write their name. Draw what they could teach you.

_____

— — — — — — — — — — — — — — — — —

My neighbor is _____ .

Focus on Neighborhood

Responsible Decision-Making

Name: _____ Date: _____

Make Good Choices

It can be hard to make good choices. It can be really hard when no one is looking. You still need to make good choices.

Directions: Read the text. Write or draw to answer each question.

You checked out a book from the school library. Your friend grabbed the book while you were reading it. A page got torn.	How would you feel?
What would you think?	What would you do?

The Right Choice

It can be hard to make the right choice. You will feel better about yourself when you do.

Directions: Read the stories. Circle the choice you would make.

1. You are supposed to walk in the halls. But no one is around. You really want to run.

   walk   run

2. Your teacher gives you some words to read. You don't know any of them.

   Try to read the words.   Pretend to read the
   Ask for help if you   words. Tell your
   need it.   teacher you are done.

3. You told Ann you would play with her at recess. Miguel wants you to play ball. You would rather play ball.

   Play with Ann.   Play with Miguel.

4. The ball bounces close to the line in handball. You see it is out. But you want to win.

   Call it in.   Call it out.

Focus on School

Self-Management

Name: _____ Date: _____

Focus on School

Social Awareness

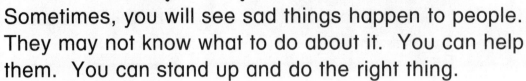

Help People Who Are Sad

Sometimes, you will see sad things happen to people. They may not know what to do about it. You can help them. You can stand up and do the right thing.

Directions: Read the story. Draw how you would help.

You are running to the swings with your friends. Marie slips and falls. Her knee is bleeding. She starts to cry. Some other students start to point and laugh. They call her a crybaby.

The Strength to Make Good Decisions

People may try to get you to do things you know are not right. Stay strong. You can still make good decisions.

Directions: Read the story. Draw what you would do. Share your answer with a friend. Tell why you made your choice.

You see a student take stickers off your teacher's desk. Your teacher sees the stickers are gone. She asks if anyone knows where they are. The student who took them looks right at you. You know he does not want you to tell.

Focus on School

Relationship Skills

Name: _____ Date: _____

Focus on School

Responsible Decision-Making

Unsafe Choices

You make choices every day. Some choices lead to good things. Some do not. Some choices may even be unsafe.

Directions: Read the story. Draw a safe choice you can make. Draw an unsafe choice.

School is over. Your friend wants you to go home with her. Your parent does not know.

Safe

Unsafe

© Shell Education

Answer Key

There are many open-ended pages and writing prompts in this book. For those activities, the answers will vary. Examples are given as needed.

Week 1 Day 3 (page 15)
top-left: happy (yellow)
bottom-left: mad (orange)
top-right: nervous (green)
bottom-right: sad (blue)

Week 2 Day 4 (page 21)
Examples may include giving the ball to someone else or playing with the ball together.

Week 2 Day 5 (page 22)
Fight with your sister and *Do not put things away* should have *X*s over them.
Help your grandparent and *Clean your room* should be circled.

Week 3 Day 3 (page 25)
Raj feels sad.
Raj feels happy.

Week 3 Day 5 (page 27)
1. Look for a kid you do not know.
2. Smile at the person.
3. Talk with the person.
4. Make a new friend.

Week 5 Day 4 (page 36)
Circle: Let everyone have a turn; You can play with us.
X: You can't play with us; We don't want to play with you.

Week 6 Day 3 (page 40)
Red: Raise your hand; Walk in a line.
Blue: Clean up dishes; Put clean clothes away.

Week 6 Day 4 (page 41)
Hands: Be still.
Eyes: Look.
Ear: Listen.

Week 9 Day 1 (page 53)
1. happy face
2. sad face
3. sad face
4. happy face
5. happy face

Week 10 Day 2 (page 59)
1. Listen to the teacher.
2. Try to do it on my own.
3. Ask for help.

Week 10 Day 3 (page 60)
Lost Tooth: a teacher, parent, or school nurse could help
Book Hunt: a librarian could help

Week 10 Day 5 (page 62)
paint spill: adult
pencil spill: child
children fighting: adult
child with zipper: child

Week 11 Day 4 (page 66)
1. trust
2. distrust

Week 13 Day 5 (page 77)
broken pencil—being handed sharp pencil
ripped paper—taping ripped paper
lunch box spill—picking up food
untied shoe—tying shoe

Week 14 Day 4 (page 81)
1. excited
2. worried
3. bored
4. cheerful

Week 16 Day 1 (page 88)
upset stomach—nervous
ready to move—happy
tired—sad

Week 16 Day 3 (page 90)
Missing Backpack—mad, sad, or worried
Birthday Surprise—excited, happy, or embarrassed

Week 16 Day 5 (page 92)
Missing Book—talk to a teacher
Birthday Party—smile and talk to friends

Answer Key (cont.)

Week 18 Day 4 (page 101)
1. angry children
2. stop sign
3. children talking

Week 19 Day 1 (page 103)
1. happy— 😄
2. loving— 😍
3. sleepy— 😴
4. surprised— 😮
5. sad— 🙁

Week 19 Day 3 (page 105)
1. both
2. internet
3. both
4. both
5. both
6. internet

Week 19 Day 5 (page 107)
Star—password
X—Pop up message; name box; continue

Week 20 Day 2 (page 109)
1. Ask to take lessons.
2. Practice throwing the ball.
3. Ask your sister for help.

Week 20 Day 3 (page 110)
1. You are really good at piano.
2. You are really good at football.
3. You are really good at building.

Week 24 Day 3 (page 130)
1. close
2. close
3. arm's length
4. very close
5. arm's length

Week 25 Day 1 (page 133)
loving—hugging
hopeful—thinking about a playground
interested—looking at an ant
confident—singing

Week 25 Day 3 (page 135)
1. thank you
2. X
3. thank you
4. thank you

Week 27 Day 1 (page 143)
Griffin: selfish, mean, unkind
Zoey: polite, helpful, nice

Week 27 Day 3 (page 145)
1. angry
2. sad
3. excited

Week 28 Day 3 (page 150)
1. confused
2. amazed
3. excited

Week 28 Day 4 (page 151)
1. teacher
2. librarian
3. brother
4. dentist

Week 28 Day 5 (page 152)
Growth Mindset: I can do hard things; I will try to get better; I can learn how to do this; I will do my best; I will try another way.
Fixed Mindset: I give up; This is too hard; I am going to make a mistake.

Week 29 Day 1 (page 153)
Lost Bike: We are sorry. We left the bike at the park.
The Garden: We are sorry. We ran in your garden.

Week 29 Day 2 (page 154)
1. Neighbors talk and decide to help.
2. Neighbors make a list of jobs to do for Mr. Withers.
3. Neighbors sign up to do jobs for Mr. Withers.
4. Neighbors take turns doing jobs for Mr. Withers.

Answer Key *(cont.)*

Week 29 Day 4 (page 156)

Responses should include Andy telling his friends that he has to stay at the park.

Week 31 Day 1 (page 163)

1. embarrassed
2. scared
3. worried

Week 31 Day 2 (page 164)

Blue: who my friends are; the way I act; the words I use; my attitude; the choices I make

Red: how people treat me; the words people say; the choices other people make

Week 31 Day 5 (page 167)

Red: Your stomach feels like it has butterflies in it; your head hurts; your hands are sweaty.

Blue: Picture a stop sign in your head; think of a happy thought; count to 10; ask for help; hug a stuffed animal; draw a picture; take a walk.

Week 32 Day 3 (page 170)

1. Ask what they are eating.
2. Take off your shoes.
3. Ask your friend about the holiday.

Week 34 Day 3 (page 180)

Responses may include that her head is down and she is away from other people.

Week 35 Day 3 (page 185)

1. sad face
2. happy face
3. sad face

References Cited

The Aspen Institute: National Commission on Social, Emotional, & Academic Development. 2018. "From a Nation at Risk to a Nation at Hope." https://nationathope.org/wp-content/uploads/2018_aspen_final-report_full_webversion.pdf.

Collaborative for Academic, Social, and Emotional Learning (CASEL). n.d. "What Is SEL?" Last modified December 2020. https://casel.org/what-is-sel/.

Durlak, Joseph A., Roger P. Weissberg, Allison B. Dymnicki, Rebecca D. Taylor, and Kriston B. Schellinger. 2011. "The Impact of Enhancing Students' Social and Emotional Learning: A Meta-Analysis of School-Based Universal Interventions." *Child Development* 82 (1): 405–32.

Goleman, Daniel. 2005. *Emotional Intelligence: Why It Can Matter More Than IQ.* New York: Bantam Dell.

Palmer, Parker J. 2007. *The Courage to Teach: Exploring the Inner Landscape of a Teacher's Life.* San Francisco: Jossey-Bass.

Name: _____ Date: _____

Connecting to Self Rubric

Days 1 and 2

Directions: Complete this rubric every six weeks to evaluate students' Day 1 and Day 2 activity sheets. Only one rubric is needed per student. Their work over the six weeks can be considered together. Appraise their work in each category by circling or highlighting the descriptor in each row that best describes the student's work. Then, consider the student's overall progress in connecting to self. In the box, draw ☆, ✓+, or ✓ to indicate your overall evaluation.

Competency	Advanced	Satisfactory	Developing
Self-Awareness	Can accurately identify one's own full range of emotions.	Identifies one's own emotions accurately most of the time.	Has trouble identifying their own feelings.
	Understands that thoughts and feelings are connected.	Sees the connection of thoughts and feelings most of the time.	Does not connect thoughts to feelings.
	Can identify strengths and areas of growth.	Can identify a few strengths and weaknesses.	Can identify only one strength or weakness.
Self-Management	Can manage stress by using several different strategies.	Manages stress with only one strategy.	Does not manage stress well.
	Shows motivation in all areas of learning.	Shows motivation in a few areas of learning.	Shows little to no motivation.
	Is able to set realistic goals.	Sets some goals that are realistic and some that are not.	Has a hard time setting goals that are achievable.

Comments

_____

_____

_____

_____

Overall

[ ]

Name: _____ Date: _____

Relating to Others Rubric

Days 3 and 4

Directions: Complete this rubric every six weeks to evaluate students' Day 3 and Day 4 activity sheets. Only one rubric is needed per student. Their work over the six weeks can be considered together. Appraise their work in each category by circling or highlighting the descriptor in each row that best describes the student's work. Then, consider the student's overall progress in relating to others. In the box, draw ☆, ✓+, or ✓ to indicate your overall evaluation.

Competency	Advanced	Satisfactory	Developing
Social Awareness	Shows empathy toward others.	Shows empathy toward others most of the time.	Shows little to no empathy toward others.
	Can explain how rules are different in different places.	Knows that some places can have different rules.	Is not able to articulate how rules may change in different places.
	Can list many people who support them in their learning.	Can list some people who support them in their learning.	Can list few people who support them in their learning.
Relationship Skills	Uses a variety of strategies to solve conflicts with peers.	Has a few strategies to solve conflicts with peers.	Struggles to solve conflicts with peers.
	Uses advanced skills of listening and paraphrasing while communicating.	Is able to communicate effectively.	Has breakdowns in communication skills.
	Works effectively with a team. Shows leadership in accomplishing team goals.	Works effectively with a team most of the time.	Has trouble working with others on a team.

Comments

Overall

_____

_____

_____

_____

Name: _____ Date: _____

Making Decisions Rubric

Day 5

Directions: Complete this rubric every six weeks to evaluate students' Day 5 activity sheets. Only one rubric is needed per student. Their work over the six weeks can be considered together. Appraise their work in each category by circling or highlighting the descriptor in each row that best describes the student's work. Then, consider the student's overall progress in making decisions. In the box, draw ☆, ✓+, or ✓ to indicate your overall evaluation.

Competency	Advanced	Satisfactory	Developing
Responsible Decision-Making	Makes decisions that benefit their own long-term interests.	Makes decisions that are sometimes impulsive and sometimes thought out.	Is impulsive and has a hard time making constructive choices.
	Knows how to keep self and others safe in a variety of situations.	Knows how to keep themselves safe in most situations.	Is capable of being safe, but sometimes is not.
	Is able to consider the consequences of their actions, both good and bad.	Is able to identify some consequences of their actions.	Struggles to anticipate possible consequences to their actions.

Comments

_____

_____

_____

_____

Overall

[   ]

Connecting to Self Analysis

Directions: Record each student's overall symbols (page 197) in the appropriate columns. At a glance, you can view: (1) which students need more help mastering these skills and (2) how students progress throughout the school year.

Student Name	Week 6	Week 12	Week 18	Week 24	Week 30	Week 36								

Relating to Others Analysis

Directions: Record each student's overall symbols (page 198) in the appropriate columns. At a glance, you can view: (1) which students need more help mastering these skills and (2) how students progress throughout the school year.

Student Name	Week 6	Week 12	Week 18	Week 24	Week 30	Week 36

Making Decisions Analysis

Directions: Record each student's overall symbols (page 199) in the appropriate columns. At a glance, you can view: (1) which students need more help mastering these skills and (2) how students progress throughout the school year.

Student Name	Week 6	Week 12	Week 18	Week 24	Week 30	Week 36

Digital Resources

Accessing the Digital Resources

The Digital Resources can be downloaded by following these steps:

1. Go to **www.tcmpub.com/digital**

2. Use the ISBN number to redeem the Digital Resources.

3. Respond to the question using the book.

4. Follow the prompts on the Content Cloud website to sign in or create a new account.

5. Choose the Digital Resources you would like to download. You can download all the files at once, or a specific group of files.

ISBN:
9781087649696

Notes

Notes

Notes

Notes

Notes